Brummie KID

More Tales from Birmingham's Backstreets

GRAHAM V. TWIST

The History Press

First published 2010
Reprinted 2011, 2012

The History Press
The Mill, Brimscombe Port
Stroud, Gloucestershire, GL5 2QG
www.thehistorypress.co.uk

British Library Cataloguing in Publication Data.
A catalogue record for this book is available from the British
Library.

ISBN 978 0 7524 5391 0

Typesetting and origination by The History Press
Printed and bound in Great Britain by
Marston Book Services Limited, Didcot

Contents

Dedication

This book is dedicated to the people who have shaped and moulded me as if I were clay. These people wrote this book as if they were doing the typing themselves: my family, my friends, my wife Sheila, fellow Summer Laners, the teachers and pupils in Cowper Street School and neighbours from Cowper Street itself, and all the good people who proudly call themselves Brummies.

Everybody I knew, looking back now into the past, had it so hard. Second-hand clothes, free school dinners, *Daily Mail* boots, fleas, nits, scabies, TB, overcoats on beds, crock hot water bottles in the cold, clammy bed (or in the case of many a family, a brick heated in the hob on the black-leaded grate and wrapped up in a cloth), the bucket on the stairs, cold lino on the floors, gas lights with mantles, huddling round the fire on freezing nights, no central heating, no hot water.

My memories of childhood are still vivid today: the chapped hands of the caring mothers slaving over the dolly and the mangle to get their kids' threadbare clothes at least clean, the pride in having her front doorstep so clean that you hardly wanted to tread on it, the spud peelings and slack thrown up the back of the little fireplace, the crooked little finger as you drank your tea out of an old enamel mug, the tea pot on the hob stewing away till the tea was almost black, the hand-made rugs, the distempered walls of the toilet that was always locked while your front door was always open, making tuppenny bundles of firewood, trying to make a few bob by hammering the oily hinges together on the only table in the room, milk poured straight out of the bottle, salmon sandwiches as a treat on a Sunday afternoon and the rabbit stew that was kept going for days. There were visits to the 'pop shop', two penny all the way round trips on the no. 8 inner-circle bus, the visits to the Lickeys, tooth-breaking toffee apples, Spanish root, Woodbines, Park Drive cigarettes sold one at a time by Vi who owned the corner shop, queueing for sweets in long lines on the one day in the year when you could get sweets without ration books, day-old bright yellow chicks from the rag and bone man. We had 5-mile walks to Perry Barr Park and then back, walks along the cut watching the barges silently pulled by the sturdy horses . . . I could go on forever but suffice to say, nobody had anything, so we were generous to a fault. If you went into a house, the first thing you were offered was a cup of tea. If you needed a hand, your neighbours would always be there. If you were sent to borrow a cup of sugar you always came back with one, and the glue that held us all together was poverty and need. Being treated worse than animals by some bosses, and ignored by most in authority – everybody was poor in their own way but they were all the richer because of it.

This book is dedicated to all those people who'll share my treasured memories and say 'Yes, that's how it was.' My fellow Brummies.

Graham V. Twist, 2010

CHAPTER ONE

Setting the Scene

It was nearly midnight, and on a cold, dark moonless night in 1958, me and my mate were crouching by a car. The car was parked on a bombed peck which was full of various different vehicles, and this bombed peck was at the bottom of Brass Street and Newtown Row in Aston. The reason we were there was because we were siphoning out the petrol from the car's tank, and why we needed that petrol was to get to work roof tiling the next day. It was almost pitch black, the only light coming from a distant streetlight in Newtown Row. We crouched there listening to the petrol dribble through the rubber tube into the 5-gallon tank. Suddenly my mate stiffened, grabbed my arm, and said, 'Sshh.' He had heard a noise – and then I heard it too, it was the ticking sound that the gears of a bicycle make when the bike is being pushed, and it was coming down Brass Street out of the blackness of the night, and more importantly, it was coming towards us. We immediately did two things: first we dropped down on the rough ground and slid under two adjacent cars, and secondly, we froze like statues. In the darkness and cold, our scared, panting breath started to condense into give-away clouds. We could hear both the ticking of the bike gears and the tinkling of the petrol which, with the combination of adrenalin and fear, was beginning to sound more and more like Niagara Falls. We lay there silently.

The bottom halves of the bike's wheels slowly came into view as did the lower legs of the pushing owner. The legs were clad in black trousers which were above black hobnailed boots and each ankle had a bike clip holding the trousers tight to those ankles. The trousers and hobnailed boots immediately told us that these were the legs of a copper, and so we lay there trying to shrink into the ground and desperately trying not to breathe. I watched the ticking wheels and police-issue boots advance towards us and the completely exposed tinkling petrol can. I thought to myself there could be no way that the policeman was going to miss seeing the can and, with a possible three years locked up in an Approved School looming, I gestured to my mate to get ready to do a runner. The half-wheels and the boots made their way past the van and suddenly and quietly the copper parked his bike up against an adjacent car. Thinking 'this is it', I shuffled to the other side of the vehicle ready for the mad race that was surely about to start. The legs sidled behind a car and stopped; there was no sound at all now – the petrol tank had obviously been drained and the can had filled up. The arcing stream of steaming piss when it hit the floor was as much a relief to us as it was to the copper, and I hit my head on the underside of the car trying not to laugh. We lay there waiting for the flood to stop, which it finally did with a satisfying 'Ahh' from the copper. He grabbed his bike, swung his piss-free leg over the crossbar and jauntily rode off into the night.

Free from the long arm of the law, we grabbed the can and were off in a flash up Ormond Street where we had digs in the attic of my sister's place. We put the can in the brewhouse up the yard where we kept our Dawes Double Blue bikes and then, still shaking with both relief and laughter, went off to bed.

Nicking the petrol when it was only 2s 3d a gallon may have seemed petty, but we were seventeen years old and couldn't have cared less. We worked for ourselves sub-contracting at tiling roofs for the Marley Tile Company which was based near Burton upon Trent and the world was our oyster. When we got a cheque for our work it would be cashed and spent on the necessities of life, like days off, fags, snooker, booze, the flicks, clothes and other important items. Hence the reason for pinching the petrol.

Me and my mate had been friends since about 1950. He had lived at the bottom end of Cowper Street in Aston and I lived up the other end of the street over the chemist's shop in Summer Lane. We had become mates because he blacked one of my eyes after some older lads had goaded us on to fight each other one day by Blews Street Park, just off Newtown Row. After the fight, which incidentally he won, he cried, I cried, and we both walked home with our arms around each other's shoulders swearing we would be mates for life, and that was how it was. His mom was a nice little woman who was always making jumpers and cardigans for him so that sometimes he looked like a little mommy's boy. Nothing could have been further from the truth. I think I must have thought of him as a bit posh because he never had anything second-hand, like shoes or clothes, whereas I was dressed up in hand-me-downs or clobber and used footwear bought from the Salvation Army place up by Gosta Green. He didn't seem to hold that against me and we got on a treat and in no time at all were inseparable – we would gee each other up to do things and seemed to be forever in some trouble or other, but none of it really bad stuff.

◆ ◆ ◆

Although I didn't know it at the time, my eldest brother's future wife, Lorraine Turton, lived at no. 3 Park Grove with her mom and dad, Evelyn and Ted. Lorraine's mom and dad had a classic wartime romance; Ted was part of an all enlisted squad that looked after the barrage balloon that was flying over Blews Street Park in the early days of the war. He and his fellow members of the squad had been billeted at no. 4 Park Grove. He obviously took a shine to Evelyn and would take her courting on their 'monkey run' down Newtown Row. As Evelyn remembers it, they would turn left out of Park Grove into Ashford Street to the corner and left again into St Stevens Street, up to Newtown Row facing Ormond Street with Asbury's the flower shop on the corner. Keeping on the left-hand side of the horse road they would pass the big café, some little houses and then Spilsburys clothes shop on the corner of Cowper Street, where all the local moms would have their Christmas clubs to save up and spend on their kids' 'best Sunday clothes'. Crossing Cowper Street, there were some terraced houses where my friend used to live, and there was a little sweet shop which was next to Bob and Agnes Jones' tobacconists and paper shop. Then there was another shop before O'Neal's second-hand shop, whose front window display would be visited by me and my mate in the future.

Evelyn and Ted would then cross Milton Street with Barclays bank on the corner and Mr Burbridge's barber shop next door, before passing the flat-windowed Stork pub and the little garage with two pumps, followed by Albert Lowe's fruit and veg market store before the Little Market, butcher's shop and the post office on Asylum Road. They'd saunter past the boozer on the corner and the Co-op with its grocery and butcher's, the gentlemen's outfitters, the Maypole grocery shop, a ladies' clothes shop selling dresses and coats and a hardware shop just this side of Inkerman Street. Then they'd pass Gould's tailors, Perk's grocery shop, Smiths the butcher's, Griffin's fruit and veg, Blacks clothes shop, Averill's cooked meats and then, past the alleyway, a tobacconist's, bike shop, a small chemist's, another sweet shop and a small

Corporal Harold Turton outside the gates and fencing surrounding Aston's 'Disney World' of its day, Blews Steet Park.

Harold 'Ted' Turton sitting among the rubble of back-to-back houses in Park Grove, Aston, blown up by German bombers during the Second World War.

Lorraine Turton's family lived in Frankfort off Summer Lane in 1929. From left to right are Emily Spencer, Alfred Spencer, Evelyn (Lorraine's mom), Eliza and Elizabeth.

jeweller's before reaching Wrensons on the corner of New Street, opposite the salubrious, no-frills-attached Globe Cinema.

Sometimes they would walk on the right-hand side of Newtown Row from St Stevens Street, past the huge Leopold Lazarus factory, three or four houses, a small fancy goods shop, a little grocer's, Whites the laundry shop and past the end of Aston Brook Street with Richardson's butcher's on the corner. Then they'd pass a photographic studio, Hunts the cake shop, Johnson's sweet shop, Pawsons the jewellers, the entry to the 'Pop Shop', the Dog and Duck, Coopers the butcher's, Timpson's shoe shop, the 'House that Jack Built', Wimbush's cake shop, the Home & Colonial grocers, and onwards, past the pub on the corner of Webster Street and Newtown Row. They'd cross Burlington Street, go past Woolworth's, an opticians, the 'Elbowroom Club', 'Blacks', 'The Aston Hip' and then go up Potters Hill with the Barton's Arms on the left.

Ted came from Derby but, having fallen for the charms of his Brummie sweetheart (whose family had always lived in the Aston area), he married Evelyn and stayed in Brum thereafter.

One day in 1952 we were mooching about in Porchester Street when we noticed one of the factory's little cast-iron framed windows was broken. Looking through we could see lots of big lampshades hanging down and underneath each one was a big, fat bulb. This was just too good an opportunity to resist, and so I nipped home and got my Diana air pistol. This was a gun that when fired, the barrel would extend and you would have to push it back in to be able to fire again. We took it in turns taking pot shots at the blameless bulbs, but because of the way the gun would jump when you fired it, I don't think we even managed one hit. It was my turn at the window and I was just taking careful aim in preparation to fire when suddenly I found myself up in the air in the grip of a big bloke wearing a trilby hat and an overcoat. I swivelled around in his hands and saw my mate was being held just the same as me by my captor's mate. He too was dressed in an overcoat and a trilby. Overcoats and trilbies only meant one thing down 'The Lane' in those days, and that was coppers.

'What do you think you are doing?' he snarled at me.

'Nothing mister.' I replied.

'Did you break this window?'

'No mister!'

'Right, come with me up to Bridge Street police station.'

Me and my mate traipsed dejectedly up the road and I prayed our moms or anyone else from our families wouldn't see us. I began to worry again whether we would have to go to court or even worse we would be sent to an Approved School. On the way to the cop shop I had been dropping the lead pellets for the gun out of my pocket so that when we got there I had got none left.

They split us up, me in one room, my mate in another.

'Whose gun is it?' asked the cop playing with the offending article.

'It's my older brother's,' I said contritely, allowing tears to form in my eyes and slide gently down my cheek in what I hoped was a picture of abject misery and fear. The cop was having none of it – he must have seen it all working in this area of Aston, one of the roughest parts of Brum going. He came round the desk menacingly.

'How many pellets have you got?' he said, putting out his big, beefy hand.

'I only had one,' was the reply.

'Lying little bleeder,' he said and gave me a head-rattling slap around the face. He felt my pockets but obviously didn't find any more of the offending slugs. He opened the door to the passage just as my mate went flying past holding his arse where the beefy copper's mate had just planted his boot. They took us in front of the uniformed sergeant who gave us a right bollocking. He handed me back the air pistol.

'Take that back to your brother and tell your mom and dad we will be watching your house to see if it is taken out by you again.'

He knew that I would get a right whaling off my mom when I told her, and he wasn't wrong.

'Now sod off the pair of you,' he yelled, and as we made good our escape through the swing doors I heard one of them say, 'only one pellet?' followed by gales of laughter from the other coppers.

♦ ♦ ♦

Being poor when you were a kid wasn't something to really worry about – everybody was virtually in the same boat. Obviously there were degrees of poverty, as with everything in life, but even those at the top of the relative ladder of affluence living in the little terraced houses all over Brum were probably only just above the poverty line. It seems to me that it was only when we were told we were poor that we began to really think about our situation and began to react to it. So, as a consequence, money or goods of any description were eagerly sought after, and it was a well-known fact that in certain pubs around the Aston area (and no doubt all around the city), things that had fallen 'off the back of a wagon' could be purchased at a fraction of their real cost. Indeed if you were in the know you could arrange for items that were desired to fall off these obviously unsafe vehicles. For instance, there was a driver at the oven factory down the Lichfield Road who would sell anyone a brand new cooker, and he obtained these cookers by the simple expedient of loading on an extra one onto his vehicle on the given day. The really big no-no about 'borrowing gear' from anyone was never to steal off your fellow neighbours; companies or factories or well-to-do people were all fair game, but you never ever stole from your own kind. Just as much as you never squealed on your mates if you were the only one who got nicked by the cops during some nefarious deed or other. Anyone who broke this unwritten rule would be ostracised by everybody in the community and in some cases could end up putting a postcard advertisement in the local shop or asking the council for an exchange, which meant you swapped your little palace for another little palace somewhere else that suited both families.

There were ways of making money on the side and there was many a house in Cowper Street, Summer Lane and the surrounding streets that resounded to the hammering together of thousands of brass hinges. The hinges would be put on newspaper on the kitchen table and knocked together with little hammers on pieces of wood to protect the table surface. The whole family would be roped into this money-making venture and there would be no going out to play until the required amount for that day had been made. Working on putting these hinges together would leave a black stain on the fingers which in the days of carbolic soap could be hard to remove. The kids who didn't have these stains would sometimes taunt the tainted ones along the lines of 'we don't have to do "out work" like you lot,' and would therefore somehow feel superior.

Bonfire nights would find us kids desperately ripping the backs off any old settees or chairs that had been donated for the blaze – the reason being that if you were lucky, you would find a few pence down the back that had fallen out of someone's pocket.

Most streets would have a lady or two who would 'lay out' the dead. They would come in and clean up the body, put a penny over each eyelid to keep them closed, put the teeth in if need be, tie the jaws up to stop the mouth gaping open, tidy the hair and dress the corpse in their 'Sunday best'. They would sometimes do such a good job that the bereaved relatives would occasionally be heard to remark 'that's the best I've seen him look in ages.' These ladies never asked for any money but wouldn't refuse it if it were offered. Generally these same women acted as midwives in the absence of doctors or nurses, and could be relied upon in most medical emergencies.

There always seemed to some lady or other in every street who could make toffee apples, and any special occasion was marked with these culinary wonders making an appearance. They were laid out on a metal tray, the apple stuck on a bit of wood cut for the job, and with the toffee slowly oozing down the apple and forming as it cooled round, flat, razor-sharp edges, which always had to be demolished first. Eating these toffee apples for backstreet kids like us who couldn't get their hands on sweets was wonderful – the crunch of the toffee along with the goodness of the apple was the sort of thing that we would relish.

Although there were cobblers in the vicinity, our dad used to repair all our shoes and boots himself. He had a three-legged metal tool, which had three different-sized foot-like protuberances, and he would put the shoe on whichever was the nearest fit. He would then hammer the sole and heel on with little tacks, which, as they went through the leather and hit the metal plate, would be flattened. Sometimes, though, one would get missed and escape so that

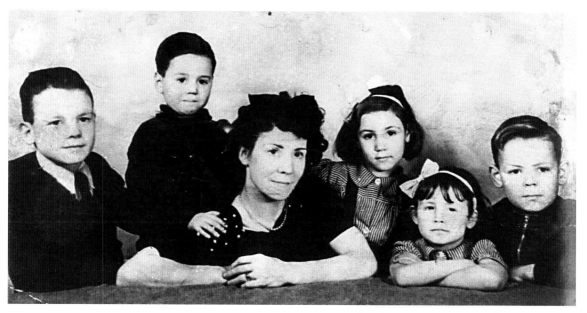

The Twist family in 1944. This photograph was taken by a professional photographer in Nechells Park Road. From left to right are Harry, Graham, May, Valerie, Yvonne and Terence.

it took its revenge for the hammering and stuck into your foot as sharp as a needle, making holes in your sock and foot with no distinction between the two. Any surplus leather sticking over the sole was cut off with a sharp knife. Our mom would darn our socks. There was a wooden mushroom-shaped tool for doing this but we couldn't even afford one of those, and as a consequence she would use a large potato inside the sock and go round and round the hole until it was all sewn up. These repairs were alright as long as the wool she used was thin, because if thick wool was used it would make a tight-fitting shoe even tighter, giving you blisters. These were not uncommon and could be really painful when you first wore the socks. I suppose this is where the saying 'you've got a spud in your sock' came from. Our mom's sewing box (an old tea caddy) contained all manner of things; there were buttons of every description, coloured ribbons, pieces of elastic, thimble mills, a little pair of scissors, and a lot of other bits and bobs. Like most women of that time she could mend, repair, cut and refashion materials of every type – absolutely nothing would go to waste. Blouses became shirts, long trousers became shorts, knitted items would be unravelled to be remade into jumpers, scarves, cardigans or even the dreaded woollen swimming nicks and costumes. These lovingly crafted items of swimwear, knitted by moms everywhere in front of their little lead-blackened grates, with their faces, noses and mottled knees burning and their backs aching with the cold, would be proffered up to the unsuspecting victim to make sure they were a good fit. These Superman-type trunks looked great in the house and many a kid was really pleased to strut their stuff wearing these fantastic-looking trunks or Esther Williams costumes at the swimming baths. Unfortunately, in the majority of cases, wearing these exotic items of swimming equipment was a one-off, and the reason soon became clear when the unsuspecting wearer entered the water for the first time. These woollen disasters would slowly begin to stretch so that lads with belts or string holding up the nicks would find it harder and harder to swim, and on being called out of the pool at the end of a session would airily (safe in the knowledge that their nicks looked great) climb the chrome ladder out of the chlorine and snot-filled green water, to the roars of derision and laughter from their fellow schoolmates, and looking down would be horrified to see that mom's work of art had stretched so that it hung down in places with the crotch far below the knees, and exposing fully his little white arse and skinny sparrow legs. Yes, it was sometimes hard to hang onto your dignity while trying to gather up this soggy, stretchy item of swimwear to cover your nudity. The girls would fare no better and would sometimes emerge from the pool with the sagging garment hanging off their shoulders and down to their waists.

I never knew anybody who had a real carpet, but there were plenty of hand-made ones in people's homes. These mats were a marvel of invention and could be any size. They were made of bits and pieces of coats or any heavy cloth cut into strips, the backing was any old sacking washed and cut to size. These improvised mats were hard-wearing, but if you didn't lift your feet when walking over them you could trip up quite easily, the strips being at least 2 inches high. When the lady of the house took the mat outside to hang on the clothes line to give it a good whacking with a broom stale or whatever else was at hand, the dust that flew out of the mat would be like a black cloud and it was best not to do it on a wash day. Most of the mats were very well made and came in all shapes and sizes and designs. I once saw one in red, white and blue which had been made to look like the Union Jack.

Before we moved to Summer Lane in the late 1940s, our family, which consisted of mom, dad, three lads, two daughters and my mom's brother, lived in Charles Arthur Street, Nechells. It was a two-up, one-down, terraced house;

one of thousands of such homes scattered around Brum. Most of these little palaces were of the same size, the only difference in a lot of cases being the amount of the occupants wedged into them.

Sharing beds was so common that no one seemed to mention it. In my case I slept in a bed with my two elder sisters until we eventually moved to 'the Lane' when I was about eight, but there were certainly other kids in bigger families that slept four and five to a bed. With rationing – no sweets, no meat (and almost no food) – the diet of the day meant that there were certainly no overweight family members, and many of the kids slept top to tail to make a bit more use of the space in the bed. The bed would sometimes have a couple of blankets and these would be directly in touch with your body – no such luxury items like sheets or pyjamas in our house. On top of the blankets could be (and generally was) anything that could possibly help to keep you warm, and these duvets of their day would more than likely be the coats and clothes you wore for school. The pillow for us three in the bed was a striped bolster. There was a little fireplace in the room but because of the beds taking up so much space it was never used, in fact it was blocked to stop the down-draught. The only heat not produced by people's bodies came from the gas outlet on the wall, which was supposed to be covered with a mantle to make the gas burn really brightly, but we rarely had one and as a consequence there were black soot marks up the wall and on the ceiling. A galvanised tin bucket on the bare wooden stairs completed the en-suite arrangements. This mobile, sometimes heavy, slopping-over receptacle was emptied every morning in your shared toilet down the yard. I don't know if it is the passage of time which has muddled my memory, but as the youngest I seemed to have more than my fair share of carrying this noxious item.

In the yards would be the toilets that two or three families shared, complete with a nail knocked into the wall supporting the string loop that carried the square pieces of toilet paper, cut from the local newspaper. These little snippets of paper could be read when nature was slow to perform, although it was also frustrating to read a piece that was interesting and then find yourself unable to find the next page. Perhaps the oddest thing about the toilets is that they always had locks on them, yet the houses were always open. Also in the yard was the brew house, a small building which housed a large copper tank built above a small fireplace. Cold water would be poured into the copper, a fire lit underneath it and away the washer would go. The sweating, turban-topped women in the yard would be there, with their aprons on, and their sleeves rolled up, scrubbing and mangling for all they were worth. Though pink-faced from the heat and the steam of the brew house, each one took a real pride in how much care they put into getting the weekly wash done, and when it was finished (if the weather was alright) the washing line would be stuck up in the air on its props, filling the yard with flapping sounds and billowing colours. The ironing of this washing in our house was always done on the living room table. Clothes would be piled up and the iron was put on the hob to heat up. To test if the iron was hot enough our mom would hold the iron base up and spit on it; if the spit crackled and shot off the iron, then it was ready.

Because everybody who lived in the yard had the same poor living conditions, and had suffered the war and its rationing, the adverse weather, having no money and all the rest of the problems that life could throw at them, the community spirit generally was very high. Of course the first loyalty was to your immediate family, so that if anyone hit 'our kid' or insulted 'our wench', he would have me and all our family to fight as well.

Harry, Terence and Valerie on 27 November 1938.

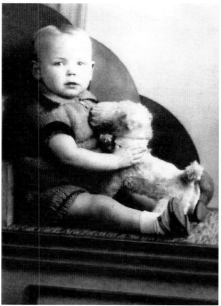

Terry in May 1937.   *Harry in December 1936.*

Sometimes if there was a dispute in the yard it could go on for ages. Outside would be turbanned women, little kids hanging onto their aprons, standing on their 'Cardinal' red coloured doorsteps, arms crossed if they were listening or hands on hips if they were arguing. I saw lots of these stand-up arguments but I never saw a punch up between the men in our yard. One person nobody ever argued with, though, was the dreaded rent man. This was a man of real importance and power, who had the authority to have any unruly family moved out and sent to the nether regions (as they were then) of Northfield or Kingstanding, and for a bloke who, say, worked in the factories of Aston, the expense and inconvenience of having to travel to his job could be a real bind. The rent man could also arrange exchanges and could get families moved to better areas. This man collected the rent from every house on his patch, in our case the princely sum of 7s 6d per week. He would also keep a close eye to make sure that the 10ft square 'garden' was tidy, the path was swept, the yard was clean, the brew house was being looked after, and that the toilets were up to scratch. This man had a lot of real power and if he had a quiet word with anyone, be it about the kids or the state of the house or anything else, you could be assured it would be acted on immediately. Unruly kids would be clouted

An entrance to a backyard behind the back-to-backs in Farm Place. Note the adverts on the walls and the entry to the 'brew 'ouse' which must have been used this day according to the washing lines. The back wall was a factory and the chimneys would have spewed smoke day and night. The noise from these factories could be anything from a low hum to massive thudding, and all the while people were living, eating and sleeping in these conditions.

May Twist in 1943.

round the head into conforming, doorsteps would be gleaming, and for weeks there would be nothing out of place. People clammed-up when he was about and tried not to stand out too much. Rent could be missed occasionally but there would be much tut-tutting and pursing of lips from him when it was.

Our mom, who used to say 'if money was a disease, I'd be in the best of health,' had somehow got hold of a mould for making wall-mounted Spanish galleons. The process was to mix up the plaster of Paris then push it firmly into the mould, insert a wire loop and the result would be a pristine white plaque that would look great on anyone's wall. My eldest brother, who thought of himself as something of an artist, would then under great duress and with copious moaning, paint the plaque. Our mom would then flog them, and all her friends and workmates seemed to have them. Another occasional little money-earner was the glass swans our dad used to make. He was a glass blower by trade and he worked six twelve-hour nights with his brother in a little factory down a back yard. These three-piece works of art, mainly blue and white in

21

colour, would be sold for the princely sum of half a crown. He could, and did, make glass walking-sticks with different colours swirling through them, and glass balls and baubles were a must for Christmas decorations. None of these entrepreneurial dealings seemed to improve our lives or living standards much; perhaps it put an extra rabbit in the pot, but it never put a new coat on your back, and we were only one household of thousands in Brum that were doing things like this to try to make ends meet.

CHAPTER TWO

Food for Thought, Fought for Food

Food was never far from our minds and seemed to be uppermost in our thoughts a lot of the time. Our mom, like everyone else's mom, was very frugal and through necessity could make a stewed rabbit last for days. This animal, looking more like a skinned cat than anything else, would be lovingly cut into bits, placed in the big black pot full of vegetables that came off a stall (and not out of a tin), with pearl barley, lentils, etc., then hung on the big hook on the black-leaded grate over the fire. The smell of this stew as it slowly cooked was wonderful, the bits of meat, stock and veggies cooking away merrily, and mom would occasionally dip in a spoon that would give you a taste of things to come. The stew would be ladled onto the chipped enamel plates to be eaten along with chunks of bread, plenty of salt, and lots of gusto. She always made sure I had a side of ribs to suck and chew on and a rabbit's kidney, this tiny oval being full of nutritious protein. If this meal was eaten on a Sunday it would be followed by my favourite rice pudding. This dessert was cooked in a black meat dish and would come out of the oven covered in a wonderful tasting black, burnt skin. Mom would cut a square chunk for us and you would put some milk and sugar on it, magnificent fare in the days of want. What was left in the pot was added to and could last another day or two. Because of the war, fresh eggs were a rarity in our house and if mom ever cracked one she always did it into a cup or onto a plate to make sure it was fresh. If it wasn't, she would take the precious object in the cup or on the plate back to the shop where she had bought it from and demanded an exchange.

Another belly-filler would be toast. When the bread went stale you could toast it and it wouldn't be too bad. We never seemed to have too much butter to spare, but you could spread it with lard topped with salt and pepper, or with jam, and eat it like that. Our dad used to like scallops and when he came home from the Beehive pub on Nechells Green on a Saturday afternoon, he would peel a couple of spuds, slice them and then fry a few scallops in the blackened frying pan, again on pieces of buttered bread with salt and pepper; I still do the same today.

One day my eldest sister came home and told our mom that the dad of a school mate of hers had got a pig in his back garden. Considering most gardens of the day in these terraced blocks were only the width of the house and about 10ft deep, this was no mean feat. Apparently he planned to hide it in the brew house when the rent man was due a visit. Anyway, he was promising anyone who helped feed the porker that they would get some fresh bacon for Christmas. This was too good a prospect to be ignored and so instead of throwing the spud peelings up the back of the fire, they were lovingly kept and religiously taken by my sister to the 'pig man' every week. Needless to say when Christmas came, this bloke would have required a street full of pigs to feed all those who had supplied him with grub for the porker, and we never even got a sniff of a rasher. The bloke and his hapless, but pork crackling-filled family, were ostracised for quite some time afterwards.

The man who lived across the yard from us had got hold of some chickens which were mostly yellow. They looked a bit strange to me as the only chickens I had ever seen close up were those at the fair or that the rag and bone man gave away for almost anything, and they were mostly multi-coloured. He had built a coop out of Outspan orange boxes and it was his intention to grow these chickens to a size where they could be killed and eaten. This man had fought through Burma and India during the war and had a photograph of himself with a monkey taken in front of the Taj Mahal, plus medals to prove it. Although he was no doubt a killing machine when it came to our country's enemies, I don't think he had given much thought as to how he was going to dispatch the innocent chickens. These chickens attracted all sorts of interested people, mostly kids, and also the very real survival interests of the local dog and cat population. You never saw a fat cat or dog back then because no one could really afford the food to give them, and these expert scavengers would scratch and claw at the box trying to relieve him of his feathered charges. He was forever running in and out of his house shouting and swearing at the attackers and trying to defend his precious Christmas dinner. Then came the fateful day of reckoning, and the

The Beehive, my dad's local, on the corner of Nechell's Place and Bloomsbury Street, Nechells.

chicken owner had enlisted me to help him. He had got one of the chickens out and tied its legs together.

'I want you to hold it upside down on the clothes line,' he said.

I managed to get the bird up to the line and clamped my hands around its claws to stop it falling. Now the 'butcher of Charley Arthur Street' showed his ruthless streak and set to work trying to cut the bird's neck. The bird must have known it was fighting for its life and it screeched and squawked madly, flapping its wings with feathers and dust flying all over the place, and all the time digging its claws into my aching hands. He must have had the bluntest knife in the world because after what seemed an eternity of sawing, swearing and chucking wobblers, he had achieved nothing, and the dishevelled chicken was still regarding me, its captor, with baleful, beady, accusing eyes. I couldn't hold the bird any longer, and we slowly lowered it to the ground. Sometime later that day I saw my hero sneaking down the yard with the chicken under his

Charles Arthur Street. We lived down on the left by the gas lamp. The shop was where I got my sweets from.

arm and later found out from his son that he had taken it to the real butcher's to be killed and cleaned. If you asked the local butcher nicely he would sometimes give you a couple of chickens' claws; you could then grip these by the anklebone and by pulling on the tendons you could make the claws open and close. In a world of few toys it was great fun (if a little macabre!).

To eat all these challenging gastronomic delights required the digestion of an elephant and the teeth of a horse, and to keep our teeth literally up to scratch our mom would wet the threadbare tooth brush, shove it up the chimney to cover it in soot, pull it down, sprinkle salt on it, and then, offering you this blackened instrument, would tell you to clean your teeth. The taste of this home-made concoction was awful, and this was supposed to do you good? It must be said that for a brief moment in time your teeth did look sparkling white, like one of the film stars we used to watch, but it was only because your gums and lips were black. Needless to say the staying power of your teeth after this enamel-removing, gum-rotting exercise would turn out to be very short-lived, and by the age of thirty me and my siblings had had most of these tortured items removed. But it was all done with your best interests at heart, by a loving mom with the magic words 'it'll do you good' so that was alright then and no one ever moaned about it.

My brother Terry had a cyst on one of his little fingers of which he seemed quite proud. I think in a drab world of sameness it made him a little bit different. When I asked our mom where he had got it from she said that when he was young he had shoved a button up his nose and that's where it had ended up. She added that if I did the same thing it might end up in the middle of my face – so no button-shoving for me, then!

Everybody seemed to have their own home cures for any problem that arose; for instance our mom would stick a red hot poker in a half pint of stout and make you drink it to cure a cold, with the words 'it'll do you the world of good,' and if tasting horrible was a prerequisite for a cure then you would never ever get another cold again. Without exception, every lad I knew had boils on their body in some place or other, but mostly on the neck. It was like your voice breaking to have one of these things on your body, almost like a rite of passage into manhood. And to get rid of the offending pus-filled pulsating hard lump, the lad's mom, dad or wise old granny would ply the very painful sensitive area with 'Black Jack' and, like a gardener waiting for a prize plant to appear, would wait until the boil had 'come to an 'ead' – usually after about ten stiff-necked, painful days. They would then, making sure the victim couldn't see it, pour some nearly boiling hot water into a small, thick glass tumbler and then place this over the blue and red throbbing half-egg-sized lump of neck-hurting boil with its fully ripe (and by now yellow) head. It was best to open the outside door and stand back at this point because as the steaming hot water cooled down, so it created a vacuum in the glass. Although the hapless victim may have been interested in the science of the whole thing at another painless time, all he knew now was that there was a demon on his back, and after frantically trying to wrench off the vampire-like pus-sucking thing of torture glued to his neck, would generally take off like a scalded cat trying to outrun it. The sight of this little ragged-arsed kid flying down the street flattening the 100-yard record, pursued by his interested peers, and sometimes barking mongrels, the poor soul screaming and clawing at his neck, must have been off-putting and even upsetting to curious onlookers, but to those in the know it was incredibly funny, with sympathy taking a very back seat.

It was said that if you had a wheezy chest or bad cold, putting goose fat onto brown paper and then placing it on the bare chest would cure it. What was not said was how uncomfortable it was walking round with a greasy, smelly, slippery piece of paper under your clothes, but it somehow seemed to work. Although, to be honest how much was cure and how much was wanting to get rid of the cure was debatable. Scabies was also sometimes a problem, and if one of the family got it then you could bet all the rest would be infected in no time. Apparently this tiny, itchy, scab-producing bug loved the warmth of the human body, so siblings all being cooped up in the same bed made them rich hunting grounds. This parasitic little mite would burrow under the rough skin on your elbows or knees, lay its eggs, and that would be the start of it. Scratching the area only made it worse and the only reliable cure for a family who had this horrible infection was to tell the council, which would then arrange for the whole family to have a special bath in some sort of sticky, smelly solution, and to let this stay on the body until it dried. It did seem to work, though.

Another home cure for a bad chest was a raw egg, mixed with pepper and vinegar. This awful combination was supposed to be drunk down in one go by the sick person. And rest assured if you weren't sick before, you certainly were after; it really was a kill-or-cure remedy. Butter and sugar mixed together and sucked would be good for a sore throat – one of the more palatable home remedies. There were dozens of different cures for different things, no National Health Service in those days, and going to see a doctor was too expensive for the working-class inhabitants of the back-to-backs.

The main reason there were so many so-called cures for chest colds and diseases was of course the terrible housing and living conditions everyone endured. Having sometimes as many as ten people stuffed into a tiny two-up, one-down, damp, wet and cold house and being forced to eat food that you wouldn't give to your dog today was a massive contributory factor to the health of the nation's working-class. We couldn't afford the grocer's prices so fresh fruit and vegetables was almost unheard of in our house, and if we were sent to buy any apples or pears our mom would say to ask him for some speckled ones, in the hope that these over-ripe things would be cheaper. We could always cut out the black bits and get stuck in.

Shared toilets and washing facilities, forty kids to a class, no hot water, no fresh air, no really warm clothing, badly leaking footwear, all these conditions made the back-to-backs a prime breeding grounds for diseases like diphtheria, bronchitis, German measles, rickets and croup. Impetigo was common among kids who lived in crowded conditions, as were stunted growth, bad eyes, rotten teeth and the worst one, tuberculosis. This killer of the poor visited itself on many an unlucky family, the child or adult slowly wasting away, coughing and spitting up lumps of phlegm and lungs in equal proportions. It didn't seem to matter how much the families of those unfortunate enough to get the disease loved them, especially the moms, or tried to care for them – without the proper treatment these blameless people were doomed in most cases to a long, lingering, slow and painful death. And although we were supposed to have won the war, rationing still lasted until the 1950s, as did all the bad living conditions we 'victors' continued to live under. Some of the lucky ones went to Switzerland in the hope of being cured; six months in the Alps on decent food and real fresh air really helped, but all it seemed to do was prolong the agony when they returned back to the conditions that had caused the illness in the first place. Most would slowly sink back into sickness before long. The council supplied bottles of concentrated orange juice and olive oil to try to combat some of the illnesses, but apart from having a different tasting drink, it didn't seem to help.

Unfortunately, despite all the best efforts with the 'tooth comb', a steel weapon of torture sold by the chemists, head lice and their eggs, the nits, were rife. These horrible little flea-like creatures were great at avoiding being caught by the meticulous grooming of your mom or your siblings through your hair, but if caught they would be squashed between the two thumbnails with a satisfying crack, similarly with the eggs. Water as hot as you could stand and skin-tenderising attacks with a scrubbing brush didn't seem to have any effect on these parasitic horrors. It was a source of great embarrassment to the family if, despite all the best efforts of the family, the 'nit nurse' found any of these bloodsucking parasites or their eggs in your hair. The nit nurse, who obviously had eyes like a hawk and seemed to be able to spot a nit from a hundred paces, was someone who came to the school at unexpected times to examine each kid's hair individually. If any nits or lice were found, the nurse would write out a report for the school and your parents, and to maximise the effect and embarrassment to the carrier, these reports were given to the kid in front of all his fellow pupils, the victim being called to the front of the class to receive the dreaded letter. Your best mates, wanting to no doubt feel superior to you, would avoid you literally like the plague for the next few days until things settled down once again. The authorities would also supply a bottle of obnoxious, evil-smelling liquid to treat the head with. In extreme cases you would be sent to the clinic to have the infestation dealt with.

Little kids, and even adults, scratching themselves was almost a sure sign of fleas. These little nasties would hide in your clothes and feed by biting the host and sucking the blood. Calamine lotion applied to the itchy area could sometimes ease the situation. If it wasn't bad enough being undernourished, unwashed and under bombs, everything creeping or crawling seemed to want some of your blood and the flat bedbug was no different from any other parasite. These little beauties would hide in the seams of the mattresses or old coats on the bed, or in cracks in the plaster on the walls. Coming out at night attracted by the heat of the body, like miniature hordes of vampire bats, they would descend on their victims, proceed to inject an anti-coagulant and pain killer and then suck out your blood. If you wanted to catch these little blood-filled pests, then a torch was the best thing. Switched on and shone around the bed you would see them in small clusters but you had to be quick to catch them. When squashed they sprayed out a mist of red blood leaving splotches wherever they had been caught, and they smelled somehow greasy. If you had to lift up the lino or the newspaper pantry shelf covers for any reason, then silverfish would scuttle all over place. Silverfish were about half an inch long and could move really fast when frightened. We also had mice in our house, God only knows what they survived on – there was certainly no excess of food hanging round our place. When I was about five I caught one by hand one day and it bit my finger and drew blood, I still have the scar now. If you had to go downstairs at night (creeping past the lurking galvanised toilet bucket) for any reason, you would sometimes hear a frantic scuttling sound, and if you were unlucky a crunching feeling under your bare foot. No slippers in those days for us, and having no electric lights it was best, if you had one, to arm yourself with a torch, or at the very least a candle. The scuttling sounds would be coming from the cockroaches that seemed to be everywhere after dark. Again it is difficult to know what they could possibly have lived off. It seems strange looking back after all this time that the thinnest and poorest of families living in terribly needy conditions could support such a host of parasites, but we did and we can thank our lucky stars that these things are less prevalent nowadays.

CHAPTER THREE

Happy Days

During the war, I, like thousands of other kids in Brum whose moms and dads worked in the factories producing the machines, bombs and bullets to kill the Germans, would have to go to the nursery. This nursery was actually a class set aside for the little kids at Cromwell Street School, Nechells. Looking after dozens of over-active kids, from eight in the morning till late in the afternoon, running around, shouting and bawling, shooting each other with imaginary six-guns or rifles, or, in the girls' case tending the wounded soldiers or cowboys, must have been a nightmare for the staff. The only means of entertainment was the big, flat, square radio with its round speaker in the middle. A bodiless voice would emanate from this radio, urging you to put your hands on your head, to sing, or walk around in some strange fashion or other – this was apparently dancing. The little girls tried seriously to follow the verbal instructions while the lads, more interested in Roy Rogers or Flash Gordon, would be playing up. The minders would do their best, but by early afternoon, having grown weary, they would get out the camp beds and try to settle these little bundles of energy down for an hour or so. I always made sure my bed, which was great to be in on my own for once, was by the window; for one so I could sneak a look out of it when the minders weren't there and two because it was close to the big, green, cast-iron heating pipes. This kip in the afternoon was great for the kids but couldn't have helped the tired, hardworking parents; fancy putting a little kid into the communal bed when they're rolling about and moaning that they can't sleep because they're not tired.

It was during one of these enforced siestas that we heard the unmistakable sound of hundreds of planes overhead. The sound was so loud that nobody could sleep, so the minders took us outside along with all the other pupils at the school to have a look. The clear blue sky was filled with what seemed like hundreds of bombers and other planes flying in loose formations. The deep, thunderous noise reverberated and made the pencils and any other loose objects in the classroom rattle and shiver. I can see it now as clear as if it happened yesterday in my mind's eye, but I don't know what it was or what they were doing to this day. In any case it certainly excited the dozens of little kids in the nursery, whose daily fare had been battles, bombs, bullets and beating the dreaded 'Jerry'.

◆ ◆ ◆

When I was about eight, my elder brother Terry, who was in the Scouts, offered to take me camping with him and his mate Trevor Murphy (who was inevitably known to one and all as 'Spud'). The venue was going to be at a far-off sounding place called Arley, down on the River Severn. He gave me an old kit bag he had got from somewhere or other and I put in my few clothes, a blanket and bits and pieces, mostly the inevitable tins of beans, the camper's friend, and whatever other stuff our mom could spare for food. It was raining when we set out; we caught the bus to town then walked to New Street station, to get the steam train that ran from Brum up to Bridgnorth. The journey was going to be on the sleep-inducing clackety train going via Kidderminster and up the length of the beautiful green Severn Valley with its meandering river, stopping at all the little stations and halts en route. By the time we got on the train it had stopped raining, so, lowering the carriage window all the way to the bottom with the strap, I stuck my head out, and with a whistle and a wave of the green flag by the guard, the pristine, snorting steam engine spun the huge wheels, slowly got a grip on the rails and we were off. There only ever seemed to be one way to travel on a steam train when you were a kid and that was with your head out of the window. I had the breath sucked out of my lungs and mouth and got bits of coal dust and steam on my face, my hair got covered in clag so that it stood up stiffly like the punks in years to come. We arrived at Arley station with a mask of black coal dust on my face and peered out through what looked like streaky, white, reverse-panda eyes. We got off the train and went across the tracks to the other side. I was struggling with my unwieldy kit bag so Spud took it off me and casually slung it on top of his own rucksack and off we went, walking along the track until we came to a stile.

'This is it!' said Terry and we climbed over the stile into the field that was going to be our home for the next week.

After we had dug out two U-shaped trenches with tiny Scout shovels, we put up the little two-man tents on the slope almost facing the Valencia pub. The trenches had been dug to regulation Scout size and shape, and were there to prevent the water running down the slope straight into the tents if it rained, which it did, and they actually worked! We settled down for the night.

'I fancy a cup of tea, go and get some water,' Terry said.

'Where's the tap?' I asked peering fearfully into the darkness of the night.

'There's no taps here! Go down there till you reach the little stream and fill the kettle there.'

I took off into the darkness at a slow pace and was soon at the stream filling the little kettle. Suddenly there was a noise behind me and spinning round with my heart in my mouth, I peered into the darkness.

'Is that you Terry?' I said, trying to sound unafraid.

A low rumbling noise was the reply from the night, followed by the sound of what seemed to be water being poured out of a jug onto the grassy bank, followed by an evil smell. What sort of unspeakable monster was out there in the darkness? Could it be a blood-sucking vampire, or was it a man-eating beast like Tarzan used to fight in the films? As a kid from the slums the only animals I had ever seen were the cart horses, and the scrawny cats and dogs that roamed our street. I was petrified and crouched low into the stingers, and that was how Terry found me half an hour later when he came looking for me with the torch he hadn't allowed me to borrow.

'Where are you?' he shouted.

'Over here!' I said, overjoyed to hear his voice in the dark. I heard him shout and wave the torch about, then there was a noise like a slow-motion stampede and then there he was with me.

'They're only cows!' he said, sounding miffed at having to come out of the tent to find me. 'Follow me back, then,' he said, and off he went, and as I followed him back to our little oasis of civilisation in this bovine-infested desert, I trod in the warm, wet mass of a fresh cowpat.

'You ain't coming in here smelling like that!' said Terry, 'go down to the river and wash it off.' I borrowed the torch and wandered dejectedly off.

Our days were spent walking the banks of the Severn, going up as far as Highley, crossing the river on the ferry, trying to catch sticklebacks by hand, and lying on our backs in the sunshine. We would shoot the flat riverside pebbles into the air with our home-made catapults, too. These stones would make a whirring sound as you shot them straight above you – it's a wonder none of us had our eyes taken out. Other days would be spent paddling and, often, pretending to be cowboys living rough in the Wild West figured quite a bit in our games. I was sitting on the bank one day fishing for our dinner. I had been given a long branch with a bit of line and a hook and been told not to come back without a fish for our tea. I didn't have a clue how to get a fish out of the river, let alone catch one, but those were my orders for the day by my scouting masters, who I now suspect had other reasons for not wanting to have me around, and so be it. I sat watching the end of the branch for ages as I had been instructed, until I got fed up and looked at the reeds. While watching them I noticed a tiny movement about a yard away; I kept my eyes on the movement and saw a dragonfly struggling to emerge from its pupa. Fascinated, I couldn't tear my eyes away. It finally broke free from its casing and, clinging on to the reed, slowly but surely began to unfurl its gossamer wings. I don't know how long it took for its wings to completely unravel, but eventually there it was, shining in the bright sunlight in all its blue-bodied glory, its four wings fluttering about. Finally, with a whirring sound like a helicopter, it majestically took off. Enthralled and willing it on, I watched it hover confidently over the water, I felt a kinship with the dragonfly having seen its birth and ready to start its airborne life, when suddenly from the left, came the blur of a bird in flight and my little blue riverside acquaintance, whose life I had seen begin, was suddenly some bird's dinner. It seemed such a shame.

One day I sat behind a fisherman who had been on the bank not far from our tent when I got up early one morning.

'What you after?' I asked him.

'Barbel,' he said, trying to ignore me.

'Do you think you'll catch one?' I asked.

'Not if you keep rattling on,' he said through clenched teeth.

I took the hint and remained quiet. After watching him getting his line caught either in the overhanging trees or tangled in the reeds, I went off. Later on I saw him standing on the bank, his rod bending and bouncing, the line as taut as a steel hawser, with the slight breeze whistling and moaning across it, and drops of river water dripping from the line as it went in and out of the water. I silently went and sat behind him to see what was going to happen. He stood there impervious to his surroundings, all his powers and energy seemed to be focussed on the whipping rod and the singing line. About half an hour later he was still in the same position and so was I; there was no way I was going to miss this Moby Dick of the mighty River Severn meeting its excited captor.

Unfortunately, as with the dragonfly, there was to be no joy for the fisherman today, because just as he was reeling in the as yet unseen and invisible monster, it hit the reeds by the bank and with one last freedom-seeking flourish it struck for deeper water. The fisherman who had got his quarry to within six feet of the bank hung onto his rod as it bent right over and then with a twang his line broke. I was glad I was up the bank at that moment because he threw his fishless rod as far as he could and his language was as ripe as some of the speckled fruit we got from the grocer's back home in Nechells. The fisherman angrily chucked all his bait into the river and wrapped up his gear, and without a second glance at me stomped off across the field to the stile, and the waiting Arley platform. Later I asked Terry if the fisherman would have eaten the fish if he had got it out of the racing rapids.

'Of course not,' he said, 'he would have put it back.'

'So why was he trying to catch it then?' I queried.

'Because it's fun and he likes doing it,' came Terry's reply.

It was then I that wondered to myself if I would ever get to understand adults.

Terry, who I am sure considered himself to be the complete all-round Scout, said to us one night, 'I am going hunting early in the morning.'

'What for?' I asked.

'Rabbits, of course!'

The next morning he left the tent as it was getting light. I crept to the entrance and watched my hero vanish into the grey mist. The only parts of him I could see were his knobbly white knees above his regulation Scout socks and boots which were leaving tracks in the cold, wet dew of early morning. How brave he was, I thought, going out all alone into that cow-filled field, trying to get food for his little brother. After about half-an-hour he came back from his Severn safari trip with a handful of rabbit fur.

'I nearly hit one,' he said. Had he got a secret arsenal?

'Hit one with what?' I asked.

'The saucepan,' he said proudly, whipping his hand from behind his back and brandishing this enamel chipped, secret, rabbit-depleting weapon of mass destruction. Needless to say he probably hadn't got anywhere near them and had more than likely got the fur off the barbed wire at the top of the field. Breakfast was a ritual affair because with both of them being Scouts, they would proudly light the little cooker and put the tiny black frying pan on it and away they would go. Thankfully I never got to burn the beans or sausages as they did.

For all their worldly Scoutliness, these two Rambos of their day couldn't stop the sounds and smells of the farts that reverberated around our little tents,

Terry and his Scout group. Terry is sixth from the left in the middle row.

Terry Twist with all his Scout group in 1947. Terry is in the front row, far right.

Terry Twist (back row, centre) top middle with his Scout troop in 1947.

encouraged by our diet. In fact I would take pleasure in trumpeting like a rapidly deflating balloon, knowing they could do nothing, and as a sign of my vanishing independence. Chores had to be done to keep the camp and its surrounding area tidy, and although I wasn't a Scout, I seemed to get more than my fair share of duties to do. But I didn't mind, I was with my big brother and his mate and felt safe in their company; it was the being there that really mattered. Five glorious days later and it was back on the puffing steam train to the reality of treeless streets and gasometers and factory-filled views, the thudding night-time noises of the local works, and the soot-stained windows of the terraced houses. All so innocent then, and those treasured days with those golden lads remain with me still.

This small incursion into the natural world had been of real interest to me; the only wildlife I had seen until then had been the sparrows and pigeons and sometimes other birds that inhabited the smoke-filled skies or the carless streets, pecking at the straw and dried horse shit that adorned the roads of Nechells and the surrounding areas. If you went on a walk down the cut by Salford Park, if you were lucky, you would be able to see some ducks, and the occasional swirl in the barge-stirred murky waters of the cut of some sort of fish, generally perch or roach.

Perhaps my journey to the countryside sparked something in me because my dad used to say to our mom, 'That kid's got itchy feet,' pointing at me after the local Bobby from Bloomsbury Street police station had brought me back home for the umpteenth time. Apparently I would just wander off and go anywhere – on buses or walking, it made no difference. I just couldn't understand what he meant; I tried scratching my feet but whatever I did they still never felt itchy – strange things, adults. I now know what he meant and he was right all along: my itchy feet took me around the world to Australia, and I have worked in Algeria, Germany, Malta, India, Saudi Arabia, Bahrain, Guernsey and dozens of places throughout England, Scotland, Ireland and Wales.

The flicks on a Saturday were a must for us kids. Me and our Von would clutch a precious tanner each, the bus fare and the entrance money, and we would walk to save the bus fare from Nechells Green to the Aston Road, where we could go left for the Astoria or right for the Aston Cross, or up the hill to the Victoria. Getting us to go to the flicks was good for more than one reason. For one it got you out of your hard-working mom's hair for a few hours, allowing her to relax or to catch up on the cleaning she hadn't been able to do during the

The Globe just after it shut for good. The cheapest wooden benches in Brum, on the corner of New Street and High Street, Aston.

week because of her war work; and two, the fun value for us kids in a world of rationing, bombs and deprivation. After entering the deafening noise and darkness of the cinema, and looking at the big safety curtains for what seemed like ages, they would slowly open to the frantic yells and catcalls of the excited kids. Watching the screen through the dust and smoky atmosphere you got to see what happened to Flash Gordon, and how he would get out of the deadly Ming's clutch – which he always did. In fact Harry Houdini would have been proud to escape some of the deadly spots Flash found himself in. Would Roy Rogers, the all-singing, all-fighting, good-looking, clean-shaven, white-hatted hero outgun the black-hatted, ugly, unshaven, hairy villains, and get to ride off singing into the sunset with the girl at his side and his white bearded, moustachioed mate Gabby Hayes, toothlessly whistling in tuneless tow? What a treat!

Roy Rogers actually came to Brum and paraded on his magnificent horse Trigger, twirling his silver six-shooters. What a sight for kids brought up surrounded by huge cart horses and canal barge-pulling horses, and the drabness of the back-to-backs. Then we would have Tarzan complete with his hirsute mate Cheetah (the best actor on the screen) and he would kill another zoo-full of lions, leopards and crocodiles because he could swim fast, and lead the lost, but immaculately dressed safari hunters, complete with a silly woman who was always falling over and screaming when being chased by rubber-toothed animals, or leaning against trees that were full of deadly snakes, to safety. Come and see, all will be revealed! Then there was the seemingly indestructible Three Stooges: Larry, Curly and Moe, those eyeball-poking, nose-flattening, arse-kicking, ear-biting, hair-pulling, shouting madmen . . . how could three people get into so much mayhem? They could really make you laugh and have you, and themselves, in stitches in no time. Laurel and Hardy were a great pair, and in fact they appeared in person at the Aston Hip once. They really were great to watch: Ollie with thoughts above his station and Stan bringing him back down to earth, always getting into trouble and, with a nervous twiddle of tie by Ollie and a scratch of the head by Stan, getting back out of 'another fine mess' once more. Who could forget the inimitable Charlie Chaplin – a chirpy little bloke who could have come from any backstreet house, arse out of his bags, second-hand shoes, ill-fitting suit, battered bowler hat and bendy cane (what he couldn't do with that cane wasn't worth knowing)? What a character! He was always fighting his so-called betters, forever the optimist, taking on the whole world and beating it. This little man would stand for no nonsense from heartless bullies and he could and would take on anyone and fight his corner to the bitter end. Just a look from out of his black eyes in his sad face could make you feel sorry for him, or if he smiled, the sun shone, and the little skinny Brummie kids watching him, I am sure, felt an affinity because of always supporting the underdog. After the show we would come out into the surprising daylight, a bomb-burst of eyeball-rubbing, happy kids riding their trusty steeds off into the dusty ravines and imaginary deserts of the Aston Road and Rocky Lane.

By 1949 our two-up, one-down little palace was getting too small for us. The sleeping arrangements by then consisted of me, aged eight, and my two sisters, one aged ten and the other one aged twelve, in one bed, my mom and my brother aged fourteen shared another bed in the same room (my dad was on permanent nights glassblowing, which made these sleeping arrangements possible) and in the other room my sixteen-year-old brother shared with my mom's brother, both of them having canvas camp beds. The en-suite facilities to the bedrooms left a lot to be desired really, in as much as the toilet was a galvanised bucket halfway down the stairs on the small landing. This was placed there as an emergency piece of equipment to help with the sudden calls of nature that would sometimes happen – better than having to go down the pitch-black yard, sometimes in the pouring rain, unlock the toilet, do your business and then repeat the process in reverse. It was a trip too far in some cases. The emptying of this eye-wateringly smelly bucket was supposed to be shared out among us kids, but it was usually me who did the honours of carrying this tin toilet down the yard. Not only would it be smelly but also if there had been a lot of traffic during the night it could be heavy and, not having the strength to hold it away from my body, it would sometimes slop over and run down my legs and into my shoes. When I moaned, my eldest brother just said, 'we had to do it for you when you were little and now it's your turn to help.' It was for the family so that was it.

Our little palace had a range for its day kitchen, lit by a single gas mantle. This cooking area was at the bottom of the stairs and consisted of a large brown Belfast sink, and the water supplying this large sink came from a single brass cold water tap connected by a lead pipe and nailed above the sink. To finish it off there was a small curtain underneath the sink to hide the two brick piers which supported it. Also in this kitchen area there were some home-made shelves, made from the wood from a banana box, to put our chipped enamel crockery on, and my very own pink plastic cup. There was also a grey mottled stove, which was a basic unit with just three rings on top, and an oven. As with most back-to-backs, when you turned the little shiny brass knob and came in the front door complete with its hanging coats on nails, you entered into our lounge-come dining, come-all-living room. This room had no mats or carpets on the floor, just lino covering the uneven red quarry tiles, and was lit by the daylight coming in through the small glass-paned window with its blackout curtains. To the left of this window was a built-in cupboard where our mom used to keep the food, and try to hide the condensed milk (some hopes). The bottom of this cupboard was filled with our shoes. It also hid a small sharp knife, and when I asked our mom what it was for, she said if the Jerries had invaded it was to cut my sisters' and her throats – a stark reminder as to how things were at that time. There was floral wallpaper on the walls with a border that stopped about two feet from the ceiling – the area above the border was distempered white. We had a picture of my eldest naked brother as a baby in a big round picture frame on the wall, and the gas mantle was in this area. The main feature of this room was a black cast-iron fireplace with a brass fender in front to stop any falling red-hot embers setting fire to the lino, or, if you were lucky, just the mat. This fireplace had a hob at either side, a grate for keeping the fire in place, a black hand-made poker rested on the fender and there was a hook for hanging pots off of. The coal to keep this fire going was delivered by the horse-powered flat coal cart and carried up the yard by the leather-backed coalman. He also wore a flat cap with its Legionnaire-style flap of material hanging from the back to protect his neck. The black-faced, white-eyed coalman would empty the dusty sacks into the small cubbyhole under the stairs. Above the fireplace was a wooden mantle shelf, complete with nail holes for the optimistic Christmas stockings to hang from. This shelf was covered with a red material with tassels hanging down and had two black statuettes either end. In the middle was a large wooden-framed mirror. Because it was the centrepiece of the room, the little grate, like thousands of other little grates in exactly the same-sized terraced back-to-back houses throughout Brum, was our mom's pride and joy. Whoever had the job of cleaning it with the Zebra blacking (in its blue and white striped tin) would have to really make a good job of it. Like the red Cardinal-brushed and -polished front doorstep and window sill, it had to be as clean as possible, and kept as shiny as could be. The hook was over the centre of the fire where she hung and cooked her famous rabbit stews.

If you had the money you could get the local window cleaner to do your windows. He would carry two wooden ladders from his cart up the yard, one that tapered at the top for doing the downstairs windows and the other one bigger for doing the upstairs. He would sometimes ask the lady of the house if she had a bucket of hot water, then having finished his job, he would be away with his cart, bucket of water, complete with its chamois leathers, hanging and swinging off one of the ladders as he went along. If you couldn't afford the window cleaner then it was on a chair for downstairs, and open the window and sit on the sill to do the upstairs, making sure you pulled the window down onto your legs so you wouldn't fall out. The so-called 'front garden' of our place was a tiny piece of bone-hard dirt; it was the width of the house and about 10ft deep, so there was no chance of putting the local grocer out of business by growing your own vegetables; besides, nothing could have thrived in this tiny, barren wasteland.

In 1947 there was an incredibly bad winter. There were huge snowdrifts, in our case drifting up the yard and against the house so that when mom opened the front door she was confronted by a wall of snow. They were great days to be a kid – snowmen all over the yards, icicles as big as the kids themselves, no school, 3ft deep snow in the horse roads. It was such fun to play in, but it was really difficult to get dry, with only the little fire in the house to stand in front of and of course there were other people bigger than you who also wanted to warm themselves. So in the end, it was no more rolling in the snow. Our mom used to say the three coldest things on earth are a man's arse, a woman's legs, and a dog's nose, and who's to deny that? The fire in this room was an essential piece of equipment; without it people could have literally frozen to death, because in the hard winters the ice would form on the insides of the window panes. Legs that had been shoved up against the fireplace, mostly the ladies and girls and little boys with shorts, would acquire a mottled appearance, so everyone knew who hogged the fire. Because our dad was on permanent nights he would light the fire early in the morning so that when we got up the room wouldn't be unbearably cold. During the long winter nights when nobody in their right mind would be out, we would all camp round this little flickering multi-coloured fire, and because we had no electricity, listen to the accumulator-powered radio with its copper wire aerial nailed outside the bedroom window under the gutter. You could get the accumulators charged by taking them to a shop in Bloomsbury Street, but as with the dreaded bucket, you had to be careful how you handled them. Like the bucket, they had a tendency to leak corrosive liquid and if they did and it got on your clothes, holes would appear. If you were really unlucky, the holes would appear in you too. The radio programmes were varied, with *The Man in Black*, *Dick Barton – Special Agent* and lots of other imagination-fuelling shows. During the day, *Music while you Work* would be played while mom went about her gruelling daily chores. Mom's favourite singer was always Bing Crosby. When the radio was no good our mom would sit us all round the fire and make up stories. They could be about anything really, and were generally of an optimistic nature. She would start and then each one of us in turn would put a word in the gap she left. These tales of fancy took our little household all over the place: the Germans, the tank battles, sinking ships and other unspeakable events certainly did not inhabit those stories. All we wanted were green fields full of cattle and sheep, hot sunny days and plentiful food.

CHAPTER FOUR

A New Stamping Ground

After months of my mom badgering them, the council finally offered us a house in an area called Aston, and more specifically in a place called Summer Lane. Our mom was overjoyed as she had been born in Gee Street – just up the road from the new house – and she felt like she was going back to her roots. We moved all our belongings on a large flat-bedded cart. It only took two trips to take all our worldly belongings with us, the striped, stained mattresses and other household items on full view to all the 'nosey parkers' on the way. When we first moved in, because we only had four beds, the sleeping arrangements didn't alter for a couple of weeks until mom and dad could afford to buy us beds. On the one hand it was great having a bed to yourself, but on the other it was sometimes cold and lonely. This house, which was above the chemist's shop on the corner of Cowper Street and Summer Lane, had an unbelievable seven rooms in it; a huge room above the shop and the same size one as our bedroom above that one. There was a lounge room, a kitchen, three big bedrooms and, marvel of marvels, an inside toilet in a real bathroom. Our mom wouldn't have any truck with the bath and we carried on having baths in the oval-shaped tin one we had bought with us. The proper bath was used to keep the coal in. So it was that we went from two tiny bedrooms to three big ones with me, my brothers and my uncle sharing one. One corner of our room had built-in cupboards that went from floor to ceiling. I climbed onto the top shelf one day and found myself in the loft space which went over the other shops in Summer Lane. There were pigeons' nests, some with eggs in them, on the lath-and-plaster ceilings.

This house had real electricity in it! It was such a novelty to be able to walk into a room and just flick down a switch for there to be light, though there were no lampshades – just a bare bulb hanging down on a wire. Our big bedroom even had two light fittings in the ceiling, but when it rained we discovered the roof must have a leak in it because the brass light switch would crackle and give off little blue flashes when you turned it on. The bare floorboards in these rooms would make hollow-sounding noises as you walked about, and it was ages before we could afford any lino, furniture being more of a priority. Outside the house on the Cowper Street side we had a big single-storey flat-roofed building. This had been used in the past to stable horses but was now purloined by my brothers who were both motorbike maniacs. The last tenants of the house had allowed the little machine shop over the road to put its swarf (metal chippings and shavings) into this building so that it was mostly full of rusty, twirly bits of steel. But this building would turn out to be a good hiding place and somewhere to play cards in the future. My brothers both kept their motorbikes in there, and when my mom bought me my first bike from Duke Street police station, a large 'sit-up-and-beg', it went in there also. Duke Street police station would hold auctions every so often of items that had been lost and found, or were recovered stolen property, the owners of which hadn't been located. My mom got this bottle-green bike for me for the princely sum of 2s 3d. It had 28-inch wheels with brakes that wouldn't work in the wet, and it weighed a ton. Even with the handlebars and seat lowered I would have to jump half off it when I finally came to a stop. No matter – it was my Roy Rogers horse to freedom and I ranged far and wide over the soot-dusted hills and plains of Aston on this trusty steed.

Moving to a new area to live was both exciting and frightening at the same time; exciting because it was all so different, a new house, new people to meet, new mates to make, a new school to go to, and frightening for exactly the same reasons. The new school was called Cowper Street School, and when I went there the headmaster was Mr Powell. Powell ran that school like clockwork, and in all the years of meeting and talking to people who attended there, I have never met anyone who had a bad word to say about this headmaster or the school, a real testament to all the hard work he put into it, supported by his loyal staff. This wonderful-looking school with its three ridged roofs and tall spire was surrounded by a phalanx of green-painted, spear-shaped railings. This fence surrounded and protected the tarmac playground presumably from any naughty things the local kids could possibly get up to. There was not a blade of grass to be seen in this playground or any sort of playing equipment that I remember. The classrooms had high ceilings and there was a staircase to take you up to the upper level balcony. The balcony was where Mr Powell or other teachers would make special announcements to the gathering of rapt future Einsteins below. It was also the place where any kid that had been singled out for being good got to read out the lesson at assembly before classes in the mornings. I did this once and it was nerve-wracking looking down seeing your mates pulling faces and trying to put you off.

The tall classrooms were very light and airy with the sunshine coming through the high, many-paned windows. We had heavy-lidded desks with the scars of years of kids carving and scratching their names into them, the ink pots surrounded by an oasis of dried ink. The pens were steel-tipped and you could snap off the point leaving a couple of sharp spikes. With this modified nib forced into the end of a straw that came with the little milk bottles, and with an ink-soaked piece of blotting paper stuck on the end, it was a formidable weapon to be lobbed at your mate's open exercise book to try to cover his page with ink splotches. I tried this method of having a go at a mate's book one day, but unfortunately not being a natural dart-thrower, my aim was way off, and instead of hitting my unsuspecting mate's book I hit the girl sitting behind him in the cheek. The terrified scream she let out made the hairs on the back of my neck stand up, and would have raised the dead. In no time the class was in an uproar and overrun with concerned teachers confronted by the weeping girl with a blood red and blue ink-stained cheek. She was surrounded by her mates all trying to comfort her (and without any sense of loyalty, I thought) pointing me out as the guilty party who had nearly killed their best friend. I was mortified for two reasons; one that I had hurt someone who was totally innocent, and two because I had a real crush on this particular girl and knew instantly we would never ever get together now. The results of my dart-throwing incident were getting the stick off Mr Powell and a letter to take home to mom who also gave me a good whaling. This future romance was put on the back-burner permanently.

If you were really lucky you would have a desk by the big, green, cast-iron heating pipes that ran around the room – a treasure on cold, wet days. The blackboard would be at the front of the class, and sometimes if the teacher had a bad bit of chalk it would screech across the board with an eye-watering sound. Some of these teachers must have been champion javelin throwers in their leisure time because if you spoke out of turn or played up in any fashion, they could throw a piece of chalk with unerring aim, hitting the reprobate squarely on the nut. In some cases it would be a beanbag that came winging your way. These little square bags were supposed to be used for games, but in the hands of a good, hard thrower, they could make your arse or legs sting, and there was many a kid that went home with a red bruise on his body somewhere.

My main academic claim to fame at Cowper Street School was that I became a milk monitor. This very responsible job entailed wearing a coloured sash over your shoulder and two of you carrying the little crate of half-pint milk bottles to the different classes. The bonuses included being out of your class until you had finished, and if anyone was absent you could drink their bottle, even though you weren't supposed to. If a teacher asked you what you were doing, it was hard to plead not guilty to drinking a nicked bottle of milk through a lying white cream-covered mouth.

The kids living in Cowper Street were like kids all over the world, in as much as there were smart arses, cowardly kids, brave kids, pain-in-the-arse kids, cheeky kids, and every sort in between. When we first moved into the street, being the outsider I obviously had to earn my place in the gang of kids that generally mooched about, played football and hide and seek, etc. This was done by the time-honoured method of a fight. There were plenty of yards big and wide enough to hold these events in and if anyone saw you having a fight then in no time there would be a crowd around the pugilists, each shouting support for their hero, and being the stranger, in the beginning that hero wasn't me. Punching and wrestling moves were allowed but strictly no scratching, hair-pulling or kicking was tolerated. It wasn't quite the Marquis of Queensbury rules but it was near enough, the real sense of fair play, and never hitting your opponent when he was down was right in the forefront when you had these fights. And if one or the other didn't abide by these unwritten rules he would soon be told so in no uncertain terms. I never saw weapons of any description used in these local sort-outs. Fight over, the ragged-arsed, dirt-covered, sometimes bloodied combatants would either shake hands 'like men', or walk away with their arms around each others' shoulders declaring they would be friends for life. This friendly situation would only last a day or so before things got back to normal. One of the lads had a mongrel dog that would literally lick your wounds – there must have been something in the dog's saliva because if you could stand the dog licking and lightly nibbling your wounds, then any scratches or scabs you had on your arms or legs would be cleaned and healed in no time.

Finally, having got myself accepted into the gang, I was allowed to go with them on bird-nesting or frog-, newt- and stickleback-capturing trips. These David Attenboroughs of their day were armed with a jam jar hanging from a string loop, and a penny bamboo cane fish net would range far and near, but mostly far. The streets of Aston were not exactly renowned for their wildlife, except for the drunks found outside the numerous pubs on a Saturday night. These safari-like forages would take us from Perry Barr Park to Red House Park, the 'Lickeys' and sometimes Sutton Park.

To get to Perry Barr Park we would catch the no. 33 bus, and if there was a gang of us (which there usually was), we would try to hide one or two of the littler kids under the seats to save the fare – there always being something better to spend our hard-earned cash on. You would get off by the Boars Head, a good old pub that split the Aldridge and the College roads. This pub had grass in front of it and there was many a family that set up for a bit of a picnic on this land while the old man had a few in the pub. Going into the park you entered a completely different world. This one, instead of being filled with smoking chimneys, noisy factories and crowded streets, was an oasis of calm, where you could actually hear the birds singing. We had a lad with us who could tell what that bird was, and there were green plants and trees around, the trees having shiny green leaves instead of the dusty brown ones to be seen on the few trees around Aston. Another one of this little exploring gang could tell you what the trees were and also what the plants were and even which ones, if you were brave enough, you could eat. Wandering about in the park, we would go bird-nesting, play hide and seek, climb trees and do all the things little kids who rarely got the chance to run about with real freedom did. To get on a bus and to travel 30 minutes or so took you into another realm, from the shortened view of the black, overcrowded walls of the back-to-backs, the house windows with their thin film of coal and factory chimney dust and grime, the never-ending dull thudding, hissing and clanking sounds throughout the night, the narrow, confining streets, and the almost impenetrable cloying damp fogs, into the sunshine and cool breezes was almost painful in its difference. Here you could run as fast as your legs could take you, breathe in the fresh air with its unusual flowery aromas. The vinegary, beery, horse shit smell of Ansells' Brewery, although wonderful in its place, just couldn't compare to the roses and other multitude of flowers in their beautifully laid out technicolour beds – the magnificent heady smell of these flowers took you into an olfactory world of your own. Playing hide and seek was a must in this Tarzan's jungle of bushes, trees and long grasses. It was mostly the older, bigger lads who would do a bit of bird-nesting, although you had to look out for the 'Parkies' during this egg-stealing exercise. If you were stopped by the 'Parky' for any reason, he always made sure, as he looked into your eyes, that he patted your pockets down, thus ensuring that if you had any illicitly gained eggs on you, they went home with you in an uncomfortable white and yellow runny jigsaw of shells leaking out of your pocket and down your leg. There were times, when getting fed up of playing about in the park, someone would suggest a walk to the 'Witton' dump. This was about half a mile away from Perry Barr Park, and to get there we went out the gates, turned left past the happy imbibers downing their pints at the Boars Head, up the College Road, over the bridge on the cut, and then turn right into Moors Lane. This lane skirted the Witton Cemetery with its red high-bricked wall on the left and had playing fields on the right. A walk down the lane and you arrived at the dump on the right. It was an interesting place because sometimes the blokes working there would let you forage about looking for things, and if you were lucky you could find a toy or two among the meagre, thrown-away objects. There were rats to be seen here and they were really large ones, and a lot of our time would be spent throwing stones and things at these champion scavenging vermin and their airborne black crow mates. We would sometimes go fishing on the cut, and you could get onto the canal path at Witton or by Perry Barr Park and walk towards Great Barr. There were plenty of fish to be caught in the cut, perch and roach being the most common. The mate I used to go with most on these fishing trips lived just round the corner from Cowper Street in Newtown Row. He was one of the most generous people I have ever met; in a world of no money and very little in the way of entertainment he would lend me the tackle, buy the bait, and lead us to the canal bank and show me how to catch fish, and if you lost a hook or a float he would willingly give you ones out of his own creel. This lad's nickname was 'Deuce' and the reason for this name was that some rough, tough, building worker had blacked both his eyes. What it was over I have no idea because this lad didn't have a bad bone in his body.

Sometimes when you walked down Newtown Row you would see the shopkeepers or the assistants using a white, distemper type paint to put advertisements in their window for that day's sales or cheap items. There always seemed to be a real art in the way these people drew the words, sometimes with flowery whirls, other times just straight. I was always surprised as to how they seemed to be able to get the lettering just perfect, and most times in one go. I am sure that there must have been competitions between them as to who did the better job.

If you were really lucky you could watch a bloke painting signs on the actual shop windows themselves. I sometimes watched these people and you'd see them clean the window first, then they would set out what looked like chalk lines, and would then start to draw whatever words they were going to use.

This bloke would have a small triangular ladder for getting to the top of the windows and all his oil paints would be on a multi-coloured artist's palette. These people were the best at shop windows and it would fascinate me to watch them ply their trade.

◆ ◆ ◆

My eldest brother, Harry, like all young blokes in the early 1950s, was interested in motor bikes, and had decided to rebuild an old Ariel bike he had got hold of from somewhere or other. The problem was that, in the interest of being under cover and warm, instead of building the bike in the garage he decided to use one of the (by now) spare bedrooms. It took all one winter to get this bike back into any sort of condition, but finally, with the help of some of his mates, he did it.

Terry aged nineteen in the Royal Artillery based in Devon in 1954.

Terry aged twenty-two.

Came the day of reckoning . . . would it start? Ever the practical one, he decided that rather than taking it down two flights of stairs and being embarrassed if it didn't go, he would start it in situ. This (on paper) simple plan turned out to have a couple of minor flaws. One was that when he did, after much cursing and one-legged jumping up and down on the pedal to start the obstinate, inert piece of metal, finally did get this roaring, petrol-reeking beast going, the fumes and noise filled the whole house like thunder and it was like being at the 'wall of death', but without the excitement of the circling bikes. The other result of this venture was that all the cups, plates and saucers on the shelves below rattled their way to freedom off the wooden shelves and onto the floor. Our mom and dad were delighted. After a brief conversation with our mom he decided with the help of our other brother Terry to get the bike downstairs and out of the house.

Again the simplest plans are sometimes not the best way and so it turned out. Because of the tightness and corners of the stairs, only two people could handle the black monster. Terry, ever the brave volunteer, decided to go backwards

Terry on holiday in Margate 1960.

down the stairs with his white-knuckled hands hanging onto the handlebars and brakes. Harry was at the back holding onto the saddle for grim death. The first flight was negotiated without any problems at all, thus luring them into a false sense of security. They regained their breath on the landing.

'That was a piece of cake, we should fly the next bit!' said our kid. And fly was the operative word. The bike, which up until this time had played the game, decided it was time to assert its independence, and as they got it onto the straight section of the steep stairs it suddenly spat warm oil onto Terry's thick, yellow hair and face, setting off a threefold sequence of events. One, it temporarily blinded him; two, it made him lose his footing, letting go of the brakes and the bike; and three, it made Harry laugh so much that he lost his grip on the saddle. The bike, seeing the open door, made its bid for freedom, and it charged over Terry and out into Cowper Street startling a passer-by. Terry was injured in more ways than one: he had a cut on his hand, he was covered in oil and the brother he was trying to help was showing his sympathy by rolling around laughing.

The rolling brother was brilliant with his hands and could seemingly make anything he put his mind to. He could also paint and had a real talent for drawing cartoons like Mickey Mouse and all his gang – he painted Mickey Mouse on my gas mask for me. Once he put his talents to the test and built me a crystal radio set which I would listen to underneath my bedclothes. This battery-less tiny radio could pick up scratchy programmes via the earphones and for a while, until it got broken, it was the doorway for me into another world. When he went to the Festival of Britain in 1951 he bought me back a luminous pocket watch which could be seen in the dark and even under the blankets at night.

CHAPTER FIVE

A New School

In 1952 it was time to leave Cowper Street School and go to a senior school. My mate was going to go to Upper Thomas Street School, so that is where I put my name down for too. This state of affairs lasted right up until the time I told our mom of my plans.

'There is only one school for you my lad and that is Summer Lane.' After blarting, moaning, and threatening to leave home, I saw the error of my decision and bowed to her superior knowledge, and it was thus I found myself at that wonderful old school, Summer Lane. It was hard at first because whereas before you were a big fish in a little pond, now the boot was on the other foot. The classes averaged forty pupils each and such was the standard of the, what seemed mostly, Welsh teachers, they were always able to have time both to encourage you and, more importantly, to listen to you. This 'big school', situated on Summer Lane amid factories and back-to-back terraced so-called 'slum' houses, gave you as good a grounding for your future life as it could. With such large classes it must have been difficult, but these hardworking teachers gave their little poor-as-church-mice pupils the best chance that they could to make good in the world.

Being taught at the big school opened up new horizons for most of us. For instance you would be taken to the sports fields at Perry Hall Park off the Walsall Road on the yellow double-decker bus for football or cricket, depending on what time of the year it was. This trip to the playing fields would always be filled with noisy, excited kids looking forward to playing football with their mates,

Summer Lane School with the bike sheds on the right – I can't recall ever seeing any bikes in there though. In front of the sheds is where we would make the death-defying slides in the winter. This photograph was taken from in front of the toilet blocks and the woodwork shop would have been on the bottom right. The top floor of the building on the right was where Mr James the headmaster's office was. The only time I ever got to go there was for 'six of the best' and that certainly happened more than once.

and telling each other what and how they were going to play. Football could be a tough game, especially if it happened to rain when you got out on the field. The ball, made of real leather, would weigh a ton when it was wet, and heading it could not only be a nightmare but could also give you a dull, throbbing headache for the rest of the day if you didn't do it right. From my own painful memory this was mostly the case. Kicking this muddy heavyweight ball was almost impossible, and if you did it nowadays I am sure you would be accused of giving yourself 'self-inflicted wounds'. We would run around resplendent in our football kit, which consisted of a coloured sash over one shoulder, any

Terry Twist (middle row, first on the left), Charles Arthur Street secondary modern, 1950.

coloured shorts, skinny white legs adorned with rolled-down socks (mostly grey in colour), finished off with a pair of hand-me-down, mud-covered, steel-tipped, studded, bruise-producing, heavy Charlie Chaplin-style boots. These boots were lethal on the feet of an incompetent player, and any accidental or even intentional kick on your shins or any other part of your body was guaranteed to leave its tell-tale vivid bruise. After an hour of running round dragging the mud-laden, half-ton boots with them, the wheezing, heaving, sparrow-chested Stanley Matthewses of the future had had enough. With most of the kids done in, the trip back to school was as quiet going back as it was noisy going.

'The thwack of leather on willow' is such an iconic phrase, but it seems to lose some of its meaning when the thwack of the leather is on an unprotected arm or some other vulnerable part of a scrawny kid's body. The cricket kit, as with the football strip consisted of a coloured sash which denoted your team over your 'whites'. This didn't always work out because sometimes it would be your mate who was on the other side and as much as you might have wanted to win, at the same time you didn't want to lose your friend. They say it is a genteel game, this cricket, but it used to scare me to bits when I was the batsman. It's one thing to bowl a ball as hard as you can at somebody, gloating to yourself as you saw real fear in his eyes (and in some cases deliberately trying to hit them), but when it was you there trying to protect yourself by holding a bat that seemed about as big as a matchstick, it was a different matter. There you were, trying short-sightedly to protect yourself against a kid with a murderous intent to maim you, his arms windmilling and armed with a really hard missile (which you just knew you wouldn't be able to parry, let alone hit), and you were fearfully shouting 'barley barley' which was totally ignored both by the madman with the missile and his sniggering team-mates. Hardly a genteel sport, really. . . .

Going to Summer Lane School was a real eye-opener for me; playing soft ball rounders, bouncing balls up walls, running around and generally larking about – I was now at a school with purpose, and that purpose seemed to be to uphold the school's good name. We pupils were all instilled with the notion to try our best in anything we did, and like your family, never bring shame on it. To this end Summer Lane had some of the best footballers, cricketers and netballers around, and although I couldn't get serious about any of these games, when 'our school' played, you gave them one hundred per cent support. I found I was good at gymnastics and was encouraged by Mr Edwards and Mr Reece to improve. The gymnastics team would put on shows for the school and we even performed at Bingley Hall and the Town Hall. To train for these events we had to go to the school two nights a week for a couple of hours. Mr Edwards and Mr Reece would be totally different people on these nights, giving advice, and helping you and always cracking jokes, and for the last half-hour of these training sessions we would get all the equipment out in the hall and you would have to try to get all round the room without touching the floor – great stuff! After they had finished with us they would adjourn to the pub on the corner of New John Street West and Hospital Street and no doubt sink a few.

Apart from 'our gang' in Cowper Street, I had never been a part of a team before, so for me this was new ground. We all had to act as a team and perform with each other, and there could be fifteen kids over the wooden horse in no time. Within the group we were encouraged to develop individual skills: one of the lads could walk on his hands for ages, and my forte was the handspring. Me and a mate were eventually asked to represent our school at the Birmingham

Summer Lane School gymnastics team in about 1955. I am in the middle row, far right.

Athletic Institute. We both felt this was great but after about six months I had to drop out because of embarrassing problems associated with obtaining the proper sports clothes and footwear. We simply couldn't afford it.

Summer Lane had its own library and I can recall being in there one day when a mate showed me a couple of photographs of some German pilots standing by their aeroplanes. I remember looking at this photograph and remarking that they were just like us. The kids I was with laughed, but I was deadly serious. I, like thousands of little Brummie kids, had been bought up on a diet of Jerry this and Jerry that, and I suppose in my own mind's eye I just didn't see the Germans as looking like ordinary people. So much for the power of propaganda.

The school also had its own woodworking class and this was held at the bottom of the playground in a large wooden shed. It was run by a small, fattish bloke, who forever seemed frustrated at his backstreet charges' lack of ability to master the arts of carpentry. Each pupil had a large wooden workbench complete with a full set of both sharp and blunt instruments of torture. He would demand that the many saws and chisels be sharp enough to have a shave with, and although this was probably the right thing to do in terms of great craftsmanship, there was many a cut finger or hand to prove it wasn't always the most sensible thing. It could have been that the seeming disinterest, and indeed fear of carpentry held by my classmates, stemmed from the fact that after you had whacked your fingers with the large wooden mallet or belted your thumb with the ball pein hammers, or even sliced through your skin with a chisel, we collectively decided that the end result wasn't worth the pain. Our noses were also permanently assailed by the stinking, gut-wrenching aroma of the forever-boiling glue. We were more interested breaking up wood for the fire at home than actually sticking it together. The poor teacher certainly did his best to teach the kids from the local streets to pick up carpentry, or at least a vague idea of how to handle tools. Unfortunately, though, he had a habit of sneaking up behind lads armed with one of the fearsome wooden mallets, and smashing it down on his bench making the lad leap with fear. With this action, he would shout, 'Gather round boys,' and then make the poor kid show the class what terrible misdemeanour he had perpetrated. It was very off-putting, and any verbal complaint or show of defiance would be countered with a beefy hand giving you a real slap in the face. When we were older, me and a mate would have sneaky fags up in the wood loft; the smell of the illicit smoke being obscured by the boiling horses' hooves, and later we would nip into the shed, sign our names then go straight back out again, returning only to tick ourselves out. As in all aspects of life, some were good at carpentry, some were bad and some were indifferent to the whole scene. Belting kids and carrying on, whatever his intentions, was perhaps not the best way to stimulate interest.

Once a year there would be a trip to the seaside. This would generally either be to Weston-super-Mare or Rhyl, the two nearest seaside places to Brum. If you were lucky, you would be able to actually see the grey, cold stuff that made us an island race. But one year our class teacher actually invited us to pick a place we would like to go to, and after much map-searching and discussion (and although I don't remember it, I am sure our Welsh teacher had a bit to do with it), Aberystwyth got the vote. I was impressed at the time that we'd had a real choice in picking where we could go after all the years of 'like it or lump it'. It was going to cost the princely sum of 10s each for the fare, but as there were some months to go, it was agreed that you could pay so much per week until

Tony Jordan and Tommy Taft with interested spectators Dolly and Christie Rose. The washing on the right is outside the future Mrs Twist's dad's house, Mr Gibbons. The lamppost seen between the houses at the bottom of the yard is where we used to climb up to light our fags.

you had the full amount. Most of us paid in instalments of threepence here and a tanner there. When you went to Rhyl or Weston it took between two-and-a-half and three hours to get there, but because we had chosen Aberystwyth this time, it took over four hours – which meant we didn't get there until about noon. We were basically let loose and told to be back at the bus in three hours' time. Three hours in even such a nice place as Aberystwyth, when you had very little money, and didn't know where to go, can seem like a very long time, and so it turned out to be. The following year, dear old Weston once again got the vote.

Discipline was necessary in such a big, crowded school such as Summer Lane, and the various teachers had their own methods of dealing out punishment. There was one teacher who had a variety of canes and actually invited you to pick which one you would like to be hit with! Having had them all, I knew there was no difference in any of them, so picking one thinking they were different must have been part of the punishment. The long, swishy bamboo cane seemed to be favourite, and the slipper or pump had its moments. Whichever cane was used, the results were the same. A trembling hand held out, and if it wasn't high enough the striker would lift your hand up with the stick. Raising the cane to shoulder height and then whipping it down across your fingers, there would be an instant numbing of the fingers and as you looked at them, the blood which had been driven out of them left a white weal, with blood-red ridges on either side. The real pain of the punishment came as the blood slowly crept back into the abused digits. Three of these strikes on both hands was generally enough to keep you in line for a while. There were other equally sadistic punishments and some were administered with what appeared to be overzealous enthusiasm. The girls, for instance, would get a ruler smacked across their hands, or bare legs, and the edge of the ruler would be rapped across the back of your knuckles if you were caught farting about. The slipper (a really a large pump), certainly warmed you up. The offender was made to bend over in front of the class, his ill-fitting shorts stretched tight as the skin of a drum over his arse. The assailant stood behind and administered six of the best, three on each cheek if you were lucky, across the backside. I can assure you it certainly made your eyes water. It was always a laugh afterwards, but at the time it would be no joke. On a cold winter's day, one punishment to warm the hands up was getting the slipper across them; three on each hand would really hurt – again the blood being driven from the fingers of the offender, there was many a rough, tough 'Laner' reduced to tears after this little lot. As an instant form of punishment, a good 'slap around the trap' was sure to make you reconsider your attitude as I found out to my cost on more than one occasion.

The pain of these punishments though, could be as nothing to the torture of dancing lessons. These lessons were held in the assembly hall, and for young kids just growing up it could be a really embarrassing experience. Kids with enormous boots or sandals on the ends of legs that had minds of their own would be asked to take a girl as a partner. If, as sometimes happened, the girl was one you secretly liked, it was even worse. We clumped around holding stiff-armed onto a different-shaped soft body from the ones you had grown up wrestling and fighting with. Having a girl this close could be very nice, but at the same time, oddly disturbing. These lessons put me off dancing for ever, and I would always say afterwards that dancing was a complicated way of getting to the bar. When you had done your Fred Astaire turn with the girl and had safely got back to your mickey-taking mates, it wasn't too wise to sneak a look at your dancing partner, because in most cases she would be among her friends, hand in front of mouth, no doubt deriding your dancing skills to her mates, and all of them laughing like drains as they looked your way.

It wasn't all sticks and slippers though, and kids being kids, there were ways of getting your own back and having a laugh at the teachers' expense. We would sometimes get student teachers for a term and they were always fair game for a joke or two. One particular incident sticks in my mind. We were having a lesson one day and the student teacher was writing the questions on the blackboard with a piece of chalk which kept on squeaking down the board. He must have known it was putting his pupils' teeth on edge, but he carried on nevertheless. Us lads in the front row decided to play him up and when he was writing on the board, signalled all those behind us not to put their hands up to answer the question. He turned round with a serious, stern look on his face.

'Now who can tell me the answer to this question?'

Not a single voice spoke out or an arm twitched. He may as well have been talking to statues. He looked back at the board to see if the question he had written made sense, and it did – the kids obviously didn't get it, so he rubbed this 'impossible' conundrum off the board and started to write another. This time, we front-row troublemakers indicated to the class to all put their hands up. When he turned round and asked the question this time he was faced with a forest of waving arms and everybody shouting out, 'Me sir!' and so it went on, question after question. It only stopped when Mr James, the headmaster stood in the corridor and saw this class of brilliant one minute and thick as muck the next pupils, and came in to have a look. You didn't treat Mr James lightly: six of the best off him was not to be sniffed at as I once found out. I met this long-suffering student teacher thirty years later, and told him what had gone on. To his great credit he not only remembered it but also had as good a laugh about it, as did I. There was some leeway to be had with most of the teaching staff, but if one or the other was having an off day, then the word would be around like wildfire. I must have been somewhere else when the message was given out about our teacher for one afternoon session. It was a geography lesson and he asked 'What do we get from the Scilly Isles?' Quick as a flash I said 'silly people.' Big mistake – it was bum-warming time once again.

CHAPTER SIX

Life in 'the Lane'

I was now firmly part of the Cowper Street mob and life was just dawdling along. The summer holidays seemed so long when you were locked out of the tarmac-covered school playground and nobody had any money to go anywhere. Like thousands of other Brummie kids, we played the usual games in the street, and sometimes especially at night under the warm yellow glow of the gas lamps. Hide and seek was a favourite in the dark; if you were 'it' you had to stand still, supposedly with your eyes shut and count to an agreed number. So it would go, 'ninety-nine, one hundred – coming ready or not!' and then you would be off trying to find your hidden mates. Even in the back-to-backs there were plenty of places to hide in the darkness. Most yards had a single gas lamp lighting them, but it would still be very dark and you could get behind the miskins, on top of the yard-dividing walls, in the brew house, in the little alleys by the toilets, or even, as was me and my mates' best spots, on the roof of either the toilet or brew house. When you caught someone they were out of the game, and whoever was caught first became 'it'.

It was during one of these night-time games that I was introduced to science in a very practical way. I was lying dead-still on the top of one of the yard walls, holding my breath, when I heard the footsteps of whoever was 'it' prowling about. I completely froze and tried to shrink even more but it was no use, he must have seen me silhouetted against the night sky because the next thing I knew an unseen hand had shoved me by my shoulder, and off the wall I went. Lesson one was Newton's Law of Gravity as I went off the wall head

A great photograph showing a typical backyard – notice the 'miskins' by the 'brew 'ouse' and paper-filled 'suff' bottom right. It must have been a washday because of the full lines. The gas lamps were always a good place to tie a rope over the bars to make a Tarzan-like swinging vines. Notice the carpet ready for beating draped over the rickety fence and the little coal shovel in the lad's hand. The cat under the window represents the sum total of local wildlife.

first. Lesson two was Astronomy with all the stars I saw on my unceremonious landing – to say I saw stars wouldn't quite cover it . . . when my nose hit the blue bricks of the yard the whole world exploded in an absolutely staggering display of lights and colours, which owing to the pain I was suffering at the time, was totally wasted on me. My mates, including the anonymous 'it' (but I know who you are) took me to a woman up one of the yards who was good at sorting out injuries and mishaps. She felt my blue and red throbbing nose with its thick trickle of red blood and green snot and announced to all, 'It's broke.' I peered at her through my two black eyes.

'Can you fix it?' I asked, 'otherwise our mom will kill me.'

'I'll try,' she said, and putting her thumb and finger on top of my conk, slowly and firmly pulled down on the throbbing nose. I never heard a click or anything, but when she stopped the relief was enormous.

Football was played constantly in the street on the sharp stone-and-pebbled tarmac strip of our own pretend Wembley turf. In the time-honoured tradition, our jumpers were the goalposts. You weren't supposed to play football in the street and any sign of the bike-riding patrolling copper was enough to send you flying up the yards, scattering the girls playing with their dolls as you went. He would try to get hold of you, and if he did, he would give you a right telling-off. This we could live with though, as long as he didn't tell your mom or dad, who would be sure to give you a good whaling for 'showing them up'. These big, brave coppers, who were only doing their duty, must have all been soldiers in another life, because without exception they all seemed to have a finely honed sense of self-preservation. This mainly manifested itself on Sunday afternoons when the alcohol-charged drinkers came out of the Three Horses and wanted to have a game of football. This time the copper would have a quick look, then pass on smartly.

Hopscotch was often played by the girls, the squares marked on the pavement, throwing their piece of slate or bottle top onto square one, then hopping on one foot to the top, turning round and hopping back, picking up their marker on the way. Needless to say these games could go on for hours on end. Whipping tops bought from the 'House That Jack Built' down Newtown Row were always around. A good whipper of the hand-chalked multi-coloured tops could keep them spinning for ages. There were bomb shelters in Cowper Street, built in the middle of the yards, and these tin-doored shelters, with their red, white and blue 'V for victory' signs painted on the walls, were used as little houses for some of the girls who would build chairs and tables for their dolls out of the numerous bricks that lay around in the shelters. These shelters were

Brother Harry's future wife Lorraine Turton (on the right) with friend Barbara Wimbush outside 3 Park Grove, Ashford Street, Aston, opposite Blews Street park, in 1949.

eventually pulled down in the very early 1950s. Go-carts were a must. These Formula 1 cars of their day could, and did, come in all sizes, but whatever the size they were all made in the same way; a long plank, two sets of pram wheels (big and small if you could get them), and a piece of strong string. The cart was made by fixing the small front wheels onto a piece of wood that was bolted in the middle to the front of the long plank, while the axle on the back wheels was simply nailed to the plank. A piece of string tied to the front wheels completed the go-cart. If you were lucky and had someone who knew how to do it you could even get a wooden brake for the back wheel. These carts were great but they also had certain pitfalls, one of which was the tram lines. Because the wheels were so narrow, they could drop into the tram tracks and you'd have to stop and lift it out. If there was a tram coming, then you had to be quick!

The natural progression from go-carts was to push bikes. There were sit-up-and-beg ones like I had, and there were ones with handlebars that swept up like an American steer's horns, and of course, the dropped-handlebar-style favoured by racers, which kept your body low and avoided a lot of the wind drag. After I had been thrown over the front handlebars while riding a fixed-wheel bike, I decided that one with proper gears was the way forward.

One day, four of us were mooching around in the horse road when two lads we had never seen before rode up 'our street'. Because there were four of us, these two were immediately challenged by one of our group to vacate the area. They slowly rode up the street and turned into Summer Lane. The lad who had shouted at them was bragging how he had seen them off. Unfortunately they had only gone round the corner to pick up three more mates, and these lads were considerably bigger than us. They came down the street and stood round us.

'Who's the big mouth?' one asked. None of us said a word: loyalty, fear and not grassing on your mates had kicked in. One of the bikers eventually piped up.

'I will fight any of you bar him,' pointing at one of our little band. This bloke obviously knew who not to pick, because this lad was a boxer and although he wasn't tall he was really broad, and looked strong. No one said a word, and then they started to take the mickey out of us. I waited for the 'big mouth' to bite, but he wouldn't, so in the end, to uphold our street's honour (misguided fool that I was), I offered to take him on. The rules were quickly established: no clawing, no biting, no scratching, let your opponent get up if you knocked him over, etc.

We started in the usual fashion.

'You hit me'.

'No, you hit me first,' and then we began to shadow-box each other, flashing out straight rights and left-hand uppercuts. We must have looked good, but neither of us had landed a single blow. I didn't want to hit him in case I upset him and I think he thought the same. At the end of an uneventful round one, both of us were flushed with the exertion of trying to miss each other. By this time, quite a little crowd had formed to watch this fight to the death, and most were yelling for me. I definitely felt the weight of the street's honour on my back. We danced about and I got renewed energy from my baying fans; snarling for the crowd, I swung a vicious right and just as I did, he slipped falling towards me. Our mutual choreography was in tatters and the punch *would* have actually knocked the skin off a rice pudding, as in the mêlée, I hit him right on the point of his conk. There was a sickening crack as his nose seemed to explode and I backed off in case I had really upset him. I needn't have worried as it turned out, because in what seemed like seconds his eyes had gone black and his nose was pouring with blood. His mates shook my hand and said 'good fight' through clenched teeth as they skulked off. Many years later we started a darts club up at the Hen and Chickens on the corner of Rocky Lane and William Henry

Graham Twist, Tony, Jerry Leneghan (my sister Von's husband) and Terry Twist at the Havelock pub on Aston Road in 1962.

Street, Nechells. One night, Johnny Prescott, that great Brummie boxer who lived round the corner, was in there with a couple of his big mates. I had to squeeze past one large bloke who was as tall as me sitting and as I went to the bar I accidentally caused him to spill some of his beer.

'Sorry mate,' I said, and as I did so he stood up. He was well over 6ft tall and as wide as a barn door, so I thought to myself 'I'd better get him a pint'. When he looked down at me and said, 'I know you, you're the kid that broke my nose years ago,' I thought my end had come. Luckily, however, he put his arm round my shoulder and called out, 'Gaffer, get this man a drink.' I nearly fainted with relief.

◆ ◆ ◆

Me and my mate used to go to the George Street Baths. Our moms would give us each a tanner and a piece of soap and off we would go. Up Summer Lane, past the Bridge Street nick to New Summer Street, turn right and down to George Street. Because we were only small, we would share a bath. The bath attendant let you into the bathroom and you had about half an hour to do your bit. For me, who had only ever had baths in our oval galvanised tin one (and after everybody else in our house, so that the water was tepid and grey-coloured), to have real hot water and as much as you liked was sheer luxury. We'd have a good soak to get rid of the ingrained dirt from knees and elbows, a wash of the hair with the soap and with your eyes tight shut a quick duck of your head in the bath to swill it out of your hair and you were done. Feeling 5lbs lighter and full of vigour, we would make our way back home. One day, coming home from the baths we went exploring a bombed peck that had a wall about 4ft high at one end. My mate ran towards it shouting, 'I bet I can jump it!' Looking like a mobile windmill, he ran up to the wall and vaulted it, and promptly vanished with a yell. I ran to the wall and looked over expecting the worst. The drop was about 10ft on the other side, but somehow he had landed upright on his feet. He stood there silently looking at me.

'Blimey,' I said, 'that was lucky,' and then he pointed down at his foot, and what wasn't so lucky was the big rusty spike that was protruding through his foot, pinning it to a large piece of wood.

'I can't move my foot,' he said.

I climbed down the wall and went to help him, and it was at this moment that I found out how tough my mate really was. It took both of us standing on the piece of wood pulling and heaving at his foot to get it off the rusty piece of metal, and not once did he cry out; his only concern was that we didn't tell his mom. As far as I am aware he never told any adult about the incident but that day he earned my real respect.

◆ ◆ ◆

Some nights me and a different mate I knew who lived in Summer Lane would meet and every so often we intrepid travellers would go on the 'monkey run'. In our case this meant a walk to the bottom of Cowper Street, a turn left into Newtown Row, looking in all the shop windows, past the Aston Hip and the Barton's Arms, and the cheapest picture house in Brum, the Globe Cinema. After that we'd go to Six Ways on the opposite side of the road to the Orient and turn left into Lozells Road, meandering past the top of Chain Walk. The Lozells Road was a long road and there were plenty of shop windows for you to flatten your nose against, all the way to Hunters Road, where we'd turn left and go down to Hockley Brook, left again into Farm Street and then you were on the home run. We would stroll along, looking in windows and talking about

Summer Lane School class photograph of 1955. Back row, from left to right: B. Rudge, B. Brecknal, J. Sturney, P. Whyton, G. Loffman, M. Clarke, M. Lane, M. Timmins, B. Wright, V. Kirby, J. Shaw. Third row: Mr James (headmaster), M. Baker, P. Sanders, J. Skelding, T. Beresford, G. Jarratt, K. Doyle, B. Froggatt, O. Wilson, M. Bryant, C. Mullins. Second row: M. Lydon, J. Mahon, J. Porch, I. Morris, M. Harrison, Mrs Holder (teacher), J. Fallowfield, H. Edouarde, A. Lutwyche, G. Beet, A. Jones. Front row: R. Tait, J. Knight, R. Edwards, D. May, T. Doody, B. Caldicot, G. Twist, J. Bates. Notice my sandals with the middle strap missing.

things; what would we do when we left school? Would we ever be able to afford a motorbike? We were really only dreaming of future plans in a life that we were only just beginning but we couldn't see changing. A job in the local factory was the height of our ambitions then. No one ever told us how to get into further education, or how to perhaps leave the slums (that disgraceful word used by the middle- and upper-classes to denote people with no intelligence or hopes beyond getting pissed on a Saturday night). Getting out of the slums and owning your own house was a dream too far, and the other classes made sure you knew it. They only wanted factory fodder. But there were some back-to-back heroes, who did make it, and in the 1955 photograph of my own class taken at Summer Lane School, there are, I am very pleased to say, two lads who did make it and became wealthy and successful men.

One night when we were on the 'monkey run' it started to rain, so we decided to take a short-cut back home. We chose to go down the cobblestoned Furnace Lane, a pitch-black poorly lit back alley which started in Gower Street and took you to Porchester Street, and then to Summer Lane. The rain had eased off as we were going up a hilly bit of the alley past the back gates of the houses, and as we passed one of these gates a head suddenly appeared over the top of it. It was the head of a bloke, and not only was he ugly but he was angry too.

'You threw bricks at my house, you little bleeders!' he shouted, as we froze in fear in the wet, dripping darkness of the night.

He began to unlatch the gate and it was then that our well-honed instincts of self-preservation kicked in. Scalded cats could not have caught up with us as we flew, screaming for our mothers into the night. I heard his footsteps behind us and our fear gave us wings; he chased us down Furnace Lane to the bottom where we burst out into blessed gas lamp-lit safety. We ran into the bar of a corner pub and stood there for ten minutes trying to recover. Finally, we went out and tried, on rubbery legs, to casually walk home.

'You shouted for your mom!' my mate said. He was a bit older than me and I think he was a little ashamed that he hadn't protected me and confronted the running madman.

'So did you!' I said, 'and your mom's dead.' I never walked down Furnace Lane again in the darkness.

There were rogues who lived in the Aston area – it would be foolish to say there weren't – but desperate times equalled desperate people, and when you are living hand-to-mouth it's hard to ignore the occasional half-chance to make a quid or two. One incident in particular springs to mind. I was talking to a lad who I knew and he told me that one of his relatives who lived in Gee Street had just been to court about the non-payment of a debt for a TV, but had been acquitted – which was a bit unusual to say the least. When the law got you in its grasp it was hard to get away with anything.

'What happened?' I asked.

'Well,' he said, 'her old man said he wanted one of them new-fangled tellies, so she went up the town and ordered one off a big dealer, and the salesman said "we will deliver it next week." Came the day for the TV to be delivered and sweet as a nut the bloke rolls up in his car with the telly in the boot. "Where do you want it, missus?" he asks. "On the sideboard by the standard lamp," she tells him. "Do you want me to connect it to the socket?" he asked. "No," she said, "my old man's an electrician and he said he wants to do it himself." "OK," says the salesman, and off he went. Two months later, not having received any money at all for the TV, the company took her to court. "Why haven't you paid for this TV?" asked the magistrate. "What TV?" she says. "The one these people took to your house." "What would I do with a TV when I haven't even got electricity in the house?" The case was adjourned while the coppers investigated, and sure enough the house had only got gas in it.'

Apparently, back in court, the magistrate threw out the case and made the company pay the woman some compensation for her 'hurt feelings'.

'What had happened then?' I asked.

'It was easy.' he said. 'She borrowed a standard lamp, and put lampshades over the gas mantles, and the salesman thought she had electricity. 'Nuff said.'

There was one fiddle that I knew went on because the bloke who did it worked with me. He was married but had no kids, and so didn't mind where he lived, although his preferred places were large houses converted to flats. Two months before Christmas he would come round the building site with a catalogue, inviting you to pick whatever you wanted out of it for half price. You wouldn't have to pay him there and then but when you finally got your hands on the gear. He would take his orders and over the weeks leading up to Christmas would deliver the items as requested, and get his reward in exchange. I asked him how he did it. 'Easy, I fill in the catalogue's questionnaire, I give them a false name and I tell them a load of porkies. I always buy something from the catalogue first and pay for it in no time. When my character has been shown to be OK I then start flogging the items.'

'How do you go on with the postman?' I asked.

'Easy. My missus waits for the postman in the morning, nips down when he rings the bell and tells him "I know Mrs so and so and she has asked me to collect her parcel." After two months of this scam, they'd pack up and go somewhere else.

CHAPTER SEVEN

For Richer, For Poorer

My Furnace Lane running mate and his family lived in a house in Summer Lane that was bomb-damaged at the front, so they lived in the back part. In the yard, one of his older brothers would spend his leisure time honing his sniper skills by shooting sparrows and pigeons off the surrounding roofs. They were a big family and hadn't got a mom or dad, but they had got a tent at Holte Fleet. This tent was an old army-issue bell tent which could sleep at least a dozen and was camouflaged. I was invited to go on a camping trip with them one year and was really glad of the offer. Six weeks off school when you had no dough and nowhere to go was way too long for me – the days just became longer and longer, and more and more boring. We caught the bus to Ombersley and walked the few hundred yards to the farmhouse where the tent was kept. We rooted it out from among a load of other canvas homes and set it up on the nearby field. The next two weeks were wonderful. There were no adults to tell us what to do, we could have real log fires outside the tent, complete with freshly-stolen-from-the-field, baked hard spuds with a bit of salt on them.

Some of our days were spent walking around the local area scrumping apples and damsons to supplement the baked bean diet now and again. On this flatulence-making menu of beans and over-ripe fruit, the saying 'farting about' took on a whole new meaning.

We were right beside the mighty River Severn and there were always plenty of fishermen to watch, catching bleak before catching a pint or two at the Wharf

Inn, a place where even rough-arsed kids from Aston were welcome. We would swim below the weir where the water was fairly shallow, would-be Tarzans in their dozens larking and rolling about pretending to be fearlessly killing crocodiles or lions, and the next minute running out of the river scared shitless if something brushed against your leg under the water.

When we were in the tent at night we all huddled together for warmth, lying on our straw beds covered with tarpaulin, the clothes we stood in being our pyjamas. We used anything we could get hold of for blankets and ghost stories would be told. It was always best if you were in the middle of this heaving mass of fidgeting, scared kids, so that the ghosts or vampires, which you just knew were waiting in the black shadows, couldn't get at you. We took walks down the river in bright sunshine, not a factory or back-to-back house to be seen, no sulphurous chimney smells, no smoke or fog or relentless factory noise to keep you awake, just the slightly unnerving peace and quiet of the countryside. When it rained and pattered on the canvas of the tent, it was great to snuggle up to your neighbour, the gentle sounds of the rain sending you off in no time. For kids whose world was brick walls, grimy streets and yellow smoke-spewing factory chimneys, the smell, and the sounds and colours of the countryside were great.

Holiday over, it was down with tent and time to pack all the cooking utensils away, consisting of one black, greasy frying pan, one lidless battered kettle and a couple of chipped enamel pots. These utensils may not have been the best tools of the trade but for starving kids living rough in the deepest parts of Worcestershire, they cooked meals fit for any king.

There was a bookies called Wheelers who served the locals in our part of the Lane. This bookies was in Brass Street, from memory if you turned into Brass Street from off Summer Lane there was an entry on the right. This entry had a solid wooden door with a letterbox in it and was bolted on the inside. This was to protect the money that the bookie would take on a daily basis. What was also there to protect the bookie's takings of the hard-earned pennies of the local punters was a load of blokes hanging around the corners and doorways nearby. These blokes were almost always dressed the same; they would have on a flat cap, a muffler round the neck and either a coat or a mac depending on the weather. If, as sometimes happened, my Uncle George had a win on the horses, he would send me to collect his winnings from the bookies. You would go up the Lane turn into Brass Street and knock on the entry door, then the door would open a crack and when you showed the invisible guard the betting slip, he would let you in. To the right were a couple of steps leading into a room that had a high counter, and you would put your betting slip on this counter and when it was checked you were given the winnings. More importantly for a skint kid, the bookie would always, without fail, give you threepence or a tanner depending on the size of the winnings.

One day, a bloke who I hadn't seen before asked me to collect some winnings for him. I took his slip to the bookies, which caused a bit of bother.

'Who give you this to collect, nip?' said one of the muffler men.

'A bloke down by the Birmingham Arms,' I said. The pub in question was just down the Lane.

'Where you going to meet him?'

'At the back of the pub,' I replied.

A glance at his muffled mates and they were off.

'Here's his winnings,' he said as he handed me the money, wrapped in a piece of paper, 'and a tanner for you. Go and stand on the corner by the pub till he comes for his cash.'

I did as he said and stood there for ages but the lucky punter never rolled up. One of the runners finally came and took the paper-covered cash back off me.

'You can go home now, nip,' he said and went back up towards Brass Street. I asked my Uncle George what it was all about and the next day he told me that the bloke who had given me the betting slip had been trying to fiddle the bookie.

My Uncle George, who lived in Moseley at the railway goods yard, and who was my mom's brother, had knocked the door of our terraced house in Nechells one wet and windy day in 1946. He stood there soaking wet with his few bits and pieces and told our mom that his wife had thrown him out when she found out he had got TB. They had sent him to a sanatorium at a place called Romsley, but the TB was too far advanced to do anything with. Without hesitation, mom told him to come in and he lived with us until the day he died.

Our Uncle George was a gentle man. I never heard him raise his voice, even when we played him up if he was minding us. He would always have a pack of cards with him and was forever playing tricks with them. He also had a small blue glass bottle supplied by the hospital, and when he coughed he would spit the results into this bottle. It could be a bit off-putting at times but he was a victim of his own circumstance. Uncle George also smoked and kept his fags

Mom's brother George (standing), who stayed with us until he died, with a friend in 1929.

in a brightly coloured tartan cigarette case. I would ask him if I could have this case when he died, and he always said yes. Needless to say when he did die in our house of this awful disease, I never got to see the cigarette case. Our Uncle George's death was not uncommon inasmuch as there were lots of people who died of TB in Birmingham and right throughout the country. When Uncle George did finally pass away, it was at the end of a long, lingering, debilitating illness. He couldn't eat or see for the last days of his life, and I only hope that he knew he was with his family who loved him. He died not long after our dad, and at that time in the 1950s, we could not afford to have him buried in a proper grave. Poor Uncle George is buried somewhere in Witton Cemetery in a paupers' grave.

◆ ◆ ◆

When we had first moved into Summer Lane I had made friends with a lad who suffered from a lung disease which meant he couldn't run around like the rest of us, but he compensated for this by being good at picking the winners at the races, drawing and painting. He was also a mean marbles player. His dad owned a horse and cart and he used to deliver sacks to The Standard Gas. He had three sisters (one who I went on to marry in the future) and a brother. He, like Uncle George, but in his case at the age of sixteen, succumbed to the lung disease in 1953.

My mate and his family lived in lived in the very poshly named Burlington Place. The name was the only grand thing about this yard, because like thousands of others in Brum, it was full of terraced houses. They came complete with outside toilets and miskins and the ever-popular concrete-roofed air raid shelter. Maybe they were posh in some small way, though, because unlike the real back-to-backs, these little palaces had their own boilers in their small kitchens.

Before hanging out her precious washing, the lady of the house would have to clean the rope clothes line with a wet rag to get off the accumulated dirt from the factory chimneys and the soot from the domestic fires. The clothes line was generally attached to the house, sometimes next to the rusty galvanised used-once-a-week tin bath, by a large nail bent over to act as a hook. The other end, if you were lucky and lived by a gas lamp, would be tied around this handy bracket. If not, a piece of wood nailed to the dividing wall would act as a support. Having hung out all the washing with the small wooden pegs (sometimes bought off the 'gypsies' who occasionally came around in their colourful headscarves worn like bandanas, selling pegs and rabbits' feet lucky charms and reading the occasional teacup or palm – 'if you buy my pegs you are going to have three kids and live a rich and long life, if you don't I will put the evil eye on you and it will be all bad luck!'). The prop would be pushed up under the line to get it out of the way and to catch the wind that always seemed to blow up the yards like the canyons in the Wild West flicks.

My mom's soft warm hands, which at other times would hold you when you were scared, comb your hair or look after your cuts and scrapes, could become as cold as blocks of ice in the winter. They would crack and become itchy, and turn a swelling red or purple colour with small open sores, and the women suffered mostly in brave silence from the pain of the horrible chilblains (ah, the strength of a mothers' love).

If you walked up the yard and looked through almost any door you would probably see a big, wooden, hand-scrubbed table, complete with a newspaper covering and, more than likely, a bottle of milk, a bottle of HP sauce, a few cups or mugs and salt and pepper containers.

There were lots of people coming round like the gypsies trying to make a crust. For instance on a Sunday you would get the 'Penny winkle man'. This bloke would come up the street shouting, 'penny winkles fresh today!' and his place of business would be a two-wheeled flat cart that he pushed about. On it were the containers that kept the winkles moist. Our mom was a glutton for penny winkles and would send me down the street to get a tanner's worth which was a half-pint beer mug filled to the top. The vendor would expertly stick the winkles in a small brown bag and that would be that. If you had enough dough he also sold a full pint glass for a bob.

Another entrepreneur at the cutting-edge forefront of technology was the bloke who sharpened the scissors and knives. This man would ride around on a pushbike with a huge grinding stone attached to it, and if he got a sale for sharpening any knives or scissors he would put the bike on a stand. Then, connecting the chain to the flywheel on the stone, he would pedal so that the stone spun around. Although I don't remember specifically, this bloke must have had legs like the roadrunner, given the amount of peddalling of the bike and peddling of his wares he did.

Then there was the Indian clothes salesman. Like the ladies, he too wore a turban, but didn't seem to have any curlers peeping out from underneath it. He would come around lugging a big old case full of clothes, and he seemed to have everything in his 'Mary Poppins holdall' – it was like a bottomless pit. There would be curtains, cardigans, knickers, bras, underwear, kids' clothes and all sorts of cheap goodies, and as long as you paid weekly, he would give you credit. Another person who would give you credit was the 'Tally Man'. This was a bloke who seemed to be able to get you almost anything you wanted as regards 'off the cuff' or tailored suits for the men, and could provide the same in costumes for the ladies. He would come to your house and measure you up for whatever it was you wanted, be it for a wedding suit or a funeral. Once the outfit had been delivered, you were expected to pay for it weekly, this bloke coming around and collecting any monies due by hand himself.

The milkman and bread man plied their trade from their horse-drawn carts, the milkman's bottles noisily clattering and clinking around the streets, the bread man quiet with his rubber-wheeled cart. The horses that drew these carts and everyday essentials around the in salubrious streets of Aston would know exactly where to stop; the milkman would hop off with his wire baskets each holding a dozen or so bottles of little, fat, aluminium-capped 'past your eyes' milk or the skinnier bottle topped 'sterra'. When he went up a yard the horse would move up the street to the next delivery point. The rag and bone man was also in attendance now and again. This hopeful scavenger of all things metal and material would come round every so often on the off chance that someone was having a clear out, and he would look over the rich pickings, offering in exchange small multi-coloured chickens, a goldfish, a plaster of Paris something-or-other or even cash. This man and his whole cart full of busted old pushbikes, bits of scrap metal and rags of all descriptions, always seemed to me to smell of horse shit.

Most tradesmen, such as window cleaners, coal haulers and milkmen, used horses and carts. Here we see a builder's horse and cart.

1953 was a good and a bad year for us as a family. On the one hand there was the Coronation. This event resulted in all the streets being trimmed up, with painted gold crowns on the walls along with red white and blue 'Union Jacks'. After years of food rationing, introduced in January 1940 on almost every item of food and clothing, to see the tables filled with food and drinks was wonderful. People had saved for ages to get some money together to celebrate the crowning of our new queen. We were supposed to have won the war but it certainly didn't seem like it when bread (which had not been rationed during the war) was suddenly rationed in 1946, and potato rationing started in 1947. During the war, bacon, meat, sugar, tea, butter, jam, cheese, eggs, biscuits, milk, and sweets were all rationed. You got 66 points for clothes each year at the beginning. But even this meagre amount was cut to 48 and then to 36 in 1943. With these points – that is, if you had the money – you could get a man's shirt (5 points), a pair of shoes (5 points), a pair of knickers (2 points), a dress (7 points) and a man's suit (26 points). After rationing started, even the frills and laces on knickers were banned so the material could be saved. There were extra points for work clothes, no points were needed for second-hand clothes or fur coats, and you could get 1lb of soap, either for house use or soap flakes. It's no wonder people got scabies, nits and fleas. To stop you getting fat and filling and overcrowding your three-, four- or five-person beds, the food rations per week were as follows: sugar (3oz), milk (3 pints), meat (1lb 3oz), butter (2oz), lard/ fat (2oz), loose tea leaves (2oz), jam (2oz), cheese (1oz), margarine (2oz), sweets (3oz) and all topped off with one egg, or a packet of egg powder that made twelve eggs (although anyone eating these 'eggs', commonly called 'Pom', would beg to differ). One of the few things not to be rationed was that most staple diet of the English working classes: fish and chips. If as a kid there was ever a better meal than hot, salty, vinegary, crunchy battered real cod, surrounded by a sea of hot chips made from real potatoes, wrapped up in newspaper you could read if you wanted to, then I certainly don't know what it is. Sweet rationing finished in February 1953, just in time, strangely, for the Coronation. Rationing finally ended in 1954. Oddly, it was also accepted that rationing improved the general health of the population. You never saw too many fat people back then. So, at thirteen years old, I, like thousands of fellow Brummie kids, had always had something or other rationed – so it's no wonder we were on the lookout to make an easy quid!

After the excitement of the Coronation and 'stuffing your hodge' to your heart's content for once, it was back to reality. In early 1953 our dad, who had worked for thirty years for one boss since he was a kid, had been sacked from his glassblowing job in Phillips Street. No real reason was given, his gaffer just saying he had had enough. There was no way that he could get another job in the glassblowing industry, and so he sought help from the authorities. The local employment office told him that a builder up in Victoria Road, by Six Ways, Aston, wanted a labourer. Despite only being 5ft tall and as lean as a whippet, he went along and got the job. His job was as a brickies' labourer, and for a bloke whose whole life had been spent working in a light trade, the difference in weights between glass and bricks and concrete must have been very hard. But he stuck at it. This job was okay for a couple of months, until he fell about 3ft off a ladder and broke both his legs – the years of being in front of the glassblowing furnace had apparently made his bones brittle. After months of being in pain and plaster and having to drag himself backwards up the stairs in our house, not earning a wage, and hardly having anything to live on, and probably too much time to think, he committed suicide. He must have wanted to make sure he did it properly because he drank a cup of arsenic (which he used as part of the glassblowing process), and he then dragged himself up to the attic and threw himself head-first out of the window. The coroner's verdict was, 'suicide while the balance of his mind was disturbed.' In this land of 'one law for them and another law for us' (you never heard of the so-called upper classes committing suicide, it was always 'accidental death'), it was apparently illegal for my dad to say he had had enough. The scrimping and having his family living virtually from hand to mouth, having his pride in his work shattered, being sacked out of hand and being discarded like a thrown-away piece of rag, practically having to go through a means test for months, had finally broken him, and because of that, it broke his family too. We had got nothing in the way of help except *Daily Mail* boots and socks and free dinner tickets – the boots and socks my mom wouldn't let me wear, because 'we ain't that poor yet,' but the dinners I did have.

Because of the coroner's verdict, the Church, that wealthiest beggar of pennies and halfpennies from the poorest and neediest (and those that have nothing to give are always the most generous of people), and the richest owners of land in the country, had shown absolutely no love of mankind at all to our family, not even extending the charity of a visit of comfort for my mom and her kids in this hour of their greatest need. It was all right for these people to go on hammering home the view about the dignity of being as 'poor as a church mouse', but it was us in our thousands who were living on or just above the starvation rations and had done so for years, not them. It must have been easy to talk about 'helping the needy' in other lands, but who was helping us? And this great institution which would willingly let a little mouse into the church, on the day of my dad's funeral wouldn't allow my dad's cold and battered body in its coffin into the church, and it was left outside while the service was conducted – so much for mice, so little for men. Our mom wouldn't let me go to the funeral, so my last view of my dad was his coffin being pushed into a hearse outside our house, and then being driven off down the Lane, the blokes standing outside the Three Horseshoes and the Geach showing more compassion and sympathy to my dad than any of the so-called caring authorities, and them taking off their hats and raising their glasses in respect to my dead dad. I didn't think about it then but now I am an old man it hurts me deeply and I am not ashamed to say I am weeping as I write this, to think of the things my dad never saw – no grandchildren, none of his kids' achievements. He, at the end of his forty-five-year life, only saw despair and no light at the end of his tunnel. It grieves me to think that I and my brothers and sisters never had a chance to say 'Tara dad', and I will never know until I meet him again if he was satisfied of the way we conducted our lives, and more importantly, would he be as proud of his kids as I am of mine. I think it was at this time that I started to go off the rails a bit – nothing bad just staying out and generally playing up.

Chapter Eight

Off The Rails

Lewis's, in Corporation Street up the town, straddled the Minories which appeared to have a rubber-surfaced road area. It was a big shop; it had six floors and on top of them a roof garden. This roof garden had a small menagerie and had monkeys and parrots and a merry-go-round and things for the little kids. It also had a great view of the city of Brum. Lewis's seemed to sell everything, but most importantly to me and my mate, the sixth floor was the toy department – you could get there by the gated lift with its attendant, or the escalators which always seemed to be packed – where we would spend hours, the bulging counters being too much of a temptation to resist. I was pretty good at nicking stuff but my mate was the 'ant's pants'; we would take anything we could get up our sleeve or into our pockets. Fountain pens, pencils, pencil sharpeners, diaries, they were all fair game to us in this Aladdin's cave of nickable items. We didn't steal to order or really for gain, we just used to 'gee' each other up to see if we had got the guts to do things (it's no excuse but that's the way it was). Pimms, the pet shop on the top of the Bullring, came in for some thievery too. White mice, which were the going rage in the pet stakes at one time, were definitely stolen to order. They cost a shilling in the shop but we would just let them run up our sleeves and then walk away with as many as were required, stopping only to try and make the big white parrot outside the shop swear, and our mice only cost a tanner each. We would go down the hill into the Bullring proper, wandering around the two-wheeled stalls, looking and generally mooching about. Nothing could be liberated here, though, the stall owner watching you with knowing eyes.

Our mom took me up the Bullring once and I can remember seeing some Roy Rogers-style jeans for sale on a clothes stall. I badgered and moaned at her to buy them for me, but they were a seven and a tanner, a price just too costly, and although she wanted to get them for me, there were other more important things to spend hard-earned cash on, like food.

Sometimes there would be someone feeding the pigeons, the feathered scavengers and their littler attendant sparrow mates making short work of anything that was dropped on the ground, including the copious amounts of horse shit that always seemed to be lying around. There were times when you would see a pigeon who had flicked up a piece of bread with a hole in the middle and it would be around its neck like a white scarf, the other birds pecking away at it trying to help their fellow disadvantaged mate escape from his crumby necklace, or so I thought.

Me and my mate, probably like thousands of other kids across Brum, would get pop bottles and beer bottles and take them back to the shops for the deposit that had to be left on them when you purchased the contents. There were ways of obtaining these bottles, from relatives giving them to you to people leaving them in shop doorways, to stealing them, and it was this latter course, for the excitement (not to mention the money), that me and my mate took. When you took the bottles back to the little shops that were dotted around the backstreets, the shopkeeper would put them in a crate behind the counter and then take them out into the backyard. Trying to get into the shop to relieve him of these bottles was almost impossible without the little bell on a spring above the door ringing. Not being able to gain the rewards by a frontal attack, we would always look to get the bottles by other methods. Most of these shops had an area at the back door where the returns were kept. This area would be either fenced in by a wooden barricade complete with barbed wire lining the top, or by a brick wall crowned with broken glass shards. One misplaced hand and the results could be very painful and bloody. There is always a key to open any door and the key to the backyard forts was a heavy sack. This piece of equipment was placed over the barbed wire or the broken glass and, provided you took care about what you were doing, over you went. We would take it in turns to scale the fences.

These nefarious deeds built up our confidence but the rush of fear of getting caught began to wear a bit thin (its called an adrenalin rush nowadays), so we looked further afield to expand our criminal empire. It was at this time in the 1950s that people were starting to be rehoused and the slums were set to be pulled down. This was when our ability to climb things came to the fore. The gas meters in these back-to-backs were protected by an easily opened small brass padlock – the biggest bar to stealing from your own meter was the shame it would generate among your neighbours. Me and my mate had no such fears. Up the yard, onto the window sill, an old blunt bread knife up between the upper and lower windows and, by pulling it to either left or right, you could undo the little brass lever that held the windows shut. If we couldn't get in downstairs we would get onto the top window sill by climbing onto the fence. Once in, it was only a matter of a minute or so to find the meter, spring the lock and take out the big brown pennies the little collection box contained. There was never a lot of money in these meters – it was the excitement of the deed that mattered.

We progressed with our life of crime by breaking into a factory yard down Brass Street. We got over the wall and just wandered around and, being 'nosey parkers', when we found a lorry with the keys still in it in a shed. I said to my mate, 'I'll show you how to start this thing.' Imagining myself to be a racing driver, I sat in the cab and turned the key – big mistake. There was a huge coughing sound that reverberated off the walls; the cab was shuddering and so was I. In desperation I switched off the key – no effect at all.

'Blimey!' shouted my mate, 'let's go!' We were over the wall and gone in seconds. 'You're going to get us caught one day messing about like that,' he told me.

People nowadays think that hooking car keys from off the table via the letterbox is a new thing. Not so; we were doing it in the early 1950s and everybody else is a copycat. As you turned left into Newtown Row from Cowper Street and walked towards the Aston Hip, there were various shops on the left-hand side. One of these was a Buy and Sell shop. There was furniture in the back, and in the shop front window there were some glass shelves with ornaments and pocket watches and bits and pieces. We were walking past this shop one day with one of the lads who had been messing about with an old wire clothes hanger – he had straightened this hanger out and was using it like a whip. We stopped as usual to gawp in the shop window and for a lark he shoved the wire through the letterbox. In no time one of the lads said try to hook that watch. After fiddling about for a while he got the hang of it and we nicked a few things off the shelf, although someone walking down towards us put a stop to the activity. When me and my mate went the next night armed with a thieving coat-hanger, the owner had nailed a piece of wood across the letterbox.

As you carried on down Newtown Row there was a clothes shop called Blacks, and not too far away was a little cake shop – I think it was called Wrensons – which had a visit one night off me and my mate. It was simple; we just went up the yard, climbed over the wall, went down the cellar and we were in. I suppose I could say it was a piece of cake! We crept up the stairs and got into the shop, treading on boxes of cakes and biscuits that were on the floor. There was no money as usual, but the excitement was sky high.

Our breaking and entering careers culminated in about 1955 with us robbing the chemist's shop I lived above. As with a lot of the places then, it was so easy to get into. There were three of us and we went through our garage into the little courtyard between the house and the garage, the gas lamp in the street throwing black shadows into the yard. The door had a glass fanlight above it which was where we intended going through to enter the shop. My mate put his foot on the doorknob and got ready to climb up, and as he did his foot pushed on the door; I noticed that the bottom of the door swung in slightly showing that it was only locked at the top. We got a file from the garage and broke the fanlight. I put my hand through and felt a bolt and pulled it across and we were in. We went into the backroom of the shop, which had furniture in it, including a big desk. We tried the drawers, but no luck – my propensity for nosiness nearly gave the other two a heart attack when I switched one of the lights on to 'see if it worked.' We entered the shop itself and rummaging around found a couple of electric shavers, toothbrushes and various bits and pieces. Going back into the backroom I searched the white coat that was hanging up on the door to see if there was any money in the pockets. There wasn't, but there was a bunch of keys. I threw them on the desk and my mate picked them up and out of curiosity tried one in the drawer keyhole, and was surprised when it fitted. He turned the key and opened the drawer to reveal the cash till's drawer, and this drawer was full of cash. We had never seen so much money in one place. The razors and other items were forgotten as we gathered up our ill-gotten gains. We cleaned out the drawer and were off. The money amounted to about £150, an absolute fortune in those days. We were almost pissing ourselves with fear and excitement: fear because if we were caught a three-year stretch at an Approved School beckoned. There were plenty of kids sent down for not really doing anything wrong, but if we got away with it, the world – and no more four penny seats at the Globe – was ours. My mate always used to say, 'if they don't catch you while you are doing the theft, they won't catch you after,' and so it proved. The coppers came down from the face-slapping, arse-kicking Bridge Street police station and had a look around. They asked our mom if she had heard anything, which she hadn't, and they never bothered to speak to me. We even had an alibi each; we had been to the flicks at the Newtown Palace the night before and had saved the stubs of our tickets to prove it. Obviously this alibi wouldn't have held water had it been checked.

The top end of Cowper Street across Summer Lane. The chemist's shop which we lived above can just be seen on the far left.

Having suddenly come into a fortune it was hard not to flash it about, but we didn't and this caused its own problems; where did that money come from if you spent too much? As a cover for our sudden cash injection, me and my mate decided to get part-time jobs. I got a job sweeping out the workshop and putting outside bundles of wood for sale at a little DIY woodwork shop on the High Street, Aston, just above the Barton's Arms. The pay was about seven and a tanner a week and for that I had to go there for about an hour-and-a-half every night, and for five hours on a Saturday. The Saturday hours were a nuisance because it seemed I had loads of dough but no time to spend it. My mate went to work for a bloke in Lozells.

At this time I only had a sit-up-and-beg bike to get around on, and my mate hadn't got a bike at all. During our 'monkey run' daydreaming trips we would look at the bikes in the bike shop (I think it was called Baileys) on Six Ways, Aston, and there in pride of place hanging from the ceiling was a Dawes Double

Blue. This magnificent bike was £29 7s 6d, unobtainable to most kids, but me and my mate had the hidden slush fund. I told our mom I had saved the deposit for the bike and she went and signed the papers so I could get it, on pain of death never to show her up by missing any payments. My mate's mom did the same. These two bikes were the passport to freedom for us; every weekend we were off! Stratford, Worcester, Droitwich, Kidderminster and all points north and south were opened up for us. And when we got part-time roof tiling jobs working for my mate's brother, we pocketed the fares he gave us and rode everywhere.

There were advantages to be had by having a few extra quid. For instance when we went to the pictures, we went upstairs or had seats at the back. If the picture was an 'A' we would, in that time-honoured fashion, wait and ask any adult 'can you take us in please?' If you were lucky he or she would take your cash and get you a ticket. Once inside, of course, you went your separate ways. We found a tanner offered for this service was sometimes enough to swing a doubter's mind and was generally acceptable. When we came out we would either have a bag of chips or, if we were going 'up the town', a tanner's worth of small baked spuds with 'as much salt as you like,' sold by the bloke by New Street station, or the other one in Navigation Street at the bottom of Hill Street.

Being young, we would always be looking for a laugh, and where better to get one that looking at cartoons at the flicks. We found that we could go to the Tatler in Station Street followed by the News Theatre, each session being about an hour-and-a-half long. There was no boozing then, but you smoked yourself silly instead. Cheap orange squash, baked spuds, ice cream and exotic fags caused an unfortunate incident one night when my mate's long-suffering stomach decided enough was enough and, without ceremony, discharged itself all over the floor at the Tatler. A hasty, white-faced retreat followed and it was some time before we visited that place again.

It was also at this time that we discovered the game of snooker. There were plenty of snooker halls in the city and suburbs, mostly above Burton's menswear shops, but the main one we would go to was the one at Witton, by the island and on the corner of Witton Road. This hall had loads of tables and although you were supposed to be sixteen to play in there, a swift bob changing hands would get us in no problem. At first the bloke running the place would stick us on tables that had less nap on them than hair on Curley's head out of the Three Stooges, but again the oiling power of the tanner did its bit and we finally got onto semi-decent tables. Eventually we had had enough of this night-time ball-bashing activity, and having found roller-skating and its attendant girls we decided to go there instead. Unfortunately the practise of winding each other up was still very much to the fore and so the last night down Witton saw us walking out with pockets full of balls, looking like a chipmunk's cheeks. Who knows why we nicked them, I certainly don't. We got on the no. 7 bus outside the hall, to take us back to the Lane, and went upstairs and sat at the front. We were just complimenting ourselves on nicking the balls when there was a clattering noise of hobnailed boots on metal stairs and the bloke from the snooker hall came towards us brandishing the sawn-off butt of a cue.

'Give me my balls back,' he shouted. There was a stunned deadly silence from the other passengers as they viewed this lethal weapon wielding madman. He was followed by the interested conductor; there was no hiding place on this bus so to our great embarrassment we had to hand over our ill-gotten gains.

'Do you want me to get a copper?' asked the conductor.

'No,' said the doorman and, looking at us, he said, 'If I see you in the hall again you will get a bit of this,' brandishing his lead-loaded weapon. Then, having taken his balls in hand, he turned and went. There was a strained silence on top of the bus that lasted until we got off it opposite the Three Horseshoes, but as we went downstairs trying to avoid looking into the passengers' no doubt outraged eyes, we heard the upper level passengers break into excited chatter and I heard some bloke say, 'they certainly had more balls than they thought they had tonight!'

The attraction that got us away from our misspent youth playing snooker was the Waldorf, a massive roller-skating rink in Sparkhill, which was arrived at by taking the no. 8 inner-circle bus. The pull of the place, apart from trying to skate at a hundred miles an hour, was the birds that frequented the huge rink. These black-eyed Elizabeth Taylor lookalikes, with their tight jeans, luminous yellow, green, pink, or red socks, topped by a sweater with interesting lumps and finished off with a fly-away chiffon scarf, would sit round the tables delicately smoking their fags and drinking their pop and seemingly ignoring all the mayhem and noise that went on around them. Occasionally some of them would get up and do a leisurely lap or two around the rink, watched all the time by the circling, pimply-faced 'nearly-Teds' with their greasy hair and drainpipe trousers. If, by any chance, you fancied one of these Elizabeth Taylor clones, it was best to try to talk to her on her own because if you approached her in front of her mates it could be extremely embarrassing, and if your bungling, amateurish mating attempts went wrong or, worse still, she didn't like you, then it could be awful. Not only would you get a very public knock back, but the object of your desires would snigger behind her hand while talking to her mates or, even more ego-deflating, laugh outright into your face. It was a good job we were young and resilient otherwise it could have put us off the opposite sex forever.

If you didn't have your own booted roller-skates you could hire them at the rink. The problem with this was you would get whatever skates the bloke behind the counter threw at you, and although you would be able to skate with them, it was how you skated that made all the difference in this new world of trying to look good. It was a little difficult to look like a 'cool cat' if your skates took your legs in different directions like the future supermarket trolleys, and you found yourself doing the splits or looking as if your legs wanted to strangle each other. There was always an answer of course, and once again the greasy palm tanner came to the rescue. Armed with a decent pair of boots, courtesy of the chemist's shop raid, our skating became a breeze. What also became a breeze was the wind blowing through your hair when you were on the wrong end of a crocodile of panic-stricken kids all hanging onto each other in sheer, white-knuckled fear. This train of terror would come about when one or two brave souls would hang onto their mates' clothes in front of them and begin to skate one behind the other at some speed. This was contrary to the rink's rules and the few attendants always tried to stop it. No chance. Within a minute or so the other skaters, good or bad, would latch onto this engine. Women, kids, smart lads, and those that didn't want to risk life and limb left the arena at this stage. Not wanting to be shown up in front of your mates, or maybe a little angry at being knocked back by the ladies, and possibly to show them you had the guts to do it, you just went for it. The lads at the front of this snaking line of potential hospital fodder would go faster and faster and in tighter and tighter circles, until the G-force at the end of the crocodile would be immense. It was not unknown for the kids' skinny legs on the end of the line to leave the wooden floor at this time and if they weren't good enough skaters and hadn't got the strength to hang on, they could be sent flying into the barriers at literally breakneck speed. Broken bones were not uncommon as an end result of these mad, suicidal circular journeys. If there were injuries, the perpetrators of this runaway fiasco could sometimes be seen watching the clean-up operation by the attendant St John Ambulance men and women, tut-tutting and feigning disgust at the awfulness of the whole thing.

CHAPTER NINE

Back on Track

If you walked up Cowper Street on the school side towards Summer Lane, on the right just past the playground there was a cobblestoned alleyway that ran past the backs of the shops that were in the Lane. The first yard in this alleyway was the butcher's; the backyard had a solid wooden gate, no doubt to stop the locals nicking the numerous bones that were in the yard. What it didn't stop, though, was the ripe aroma of these bones with their bits of rotting meat pervading the area when the weather was hot. Occasionally this gate would be open, revealing the source of the eye-watering stink. I have no idea what the butcher did with the bones but I do know that the galvanised miskins he had in that yard were seething with maggots. There were bluebottles all over the place and, in the interests of science and no doubt to get our own back, we would catch these flies by hand. This was a lot easier than it sounds. You waited until a fly had landed on the wall, then carefully put your open hand about a foot behind it, and with a quick forward sliding motion you could catch the fly. You didn't get them all but, apparently, when flies take off they always go backwards, so flying into your open Venus Fly Trap-type clutching hand. Once you had your captive fly and had got it by the wings with your finger and thumb, the scientific side of the matter would take over. Along the wall there would be spiders' webs with silken tunnels that went back into the walls through the cracks in the mortar. You took your fly and carefully pushed its legs into the web where it immediately got caught. Once you knew it was captured, you let it go and stood and watched. The fly's struggles soon had the spider

The back exit from Summer Lane School. The pub the PT teachers used to frequent was to the left of the school.

poking its hungry head out of the tunnel and then, with a rapid dash across the web, it would grab the fly and start to weave it into a cocoon of web. The final act of the whole affair saw the spider taking its prized dinner back into its tunnel – gruesome, but we were only kids.

Having turned right out of Cowper Street into Summer Lane, next to the chemist's shop was the butcher's shop. Then there was a sweet shop called Dunn's and further down was a fish and chip shop. Me and my mate would spend ages in this fish and chip shop talking to the owner and his wife, and it's true to say this man was really open-minded and saw us for what we were and not what we thought we were. The fish shop flogged not only fish and chips but also faggots and peas, both of which smelled wonderful. On the counter would be the usual items like vinegar, salt, a large bottle of pickled eggs, a jar of pickled onions, and a gallon flagon of urine-coloured, diluted orange juice. This orange juice was sold at two pence a plastic cup and I must admit I didn't like it at all, but my mate had taken a liking to it and one night he had a bet with the owner that he could drink the whole lot, the bet being if he drank it he didn't pay for it but if he didn't he'd have to shell out for it. There was no time limit but it had to be drunk before the shop shut for the night. He started off and, over the next hour or so, made real inroads into the bottle. However, obviously nature began to take its course, and my mate asked, 'Can I use your toilet?' Eyeing the ever-diminishing, potentially profitless bottle, and in the interests of fair play, supporting the underdog and all that, the owner said, 'No.' We ended up going to our house for him to relieve himself. When we got back to the fish and chip shop the bottle looked suspiciously fuller than when we had left. After two hours of imbibing the orange concoction and, with only a couple of cups left in it, closing time bought down the curtain. Honours were declared even and the owner only made my mate pay for half of the flagon of juice. I think my mate used this as a training session for our later years when the orange would be changed for beer.

As a cover for our having money, me and my mate had got our part-time jobs working at different places. We then went to work Saturdays and Sundays for his brother, who was a roof tiler. He was self-employed and did all of his works for the Marley Tile Co. The jobs he had to tile were all over the place, nearly all within 25 miles and mostly in the Lichfield, Burton-upon-Trent, Tamworth and Polesworth areas. All of these places could be reached by either steam train or local bus. Our employer would give us the fares and would expect us to get to the sites by ourselves. This is where the bikes came in; we got hold of a map, got on our bikes and just went. The traffic on the roads would be very light and we would race to the sites in an hour or so.

If we had to go by train it was a matter of pride for us to do it without paying the fares. This was relatively easy provided you had the guts to do it. We would get a penny platform ticket at the station in Brum, and when the right train came along just got on it. We always got on right at the back so that when the train pulled into the little stations we would be right at the end of the platform. We would then hang around until the ticket collector had gone back inside his little office then make a dash for it or would simply jump off the platform cross the line and go out off the opposite platform. If the ticket collector caught you on the train we used to say we had got on at the last station. Having gone by coach and missing the return journey, four of us once travelled from Aberystwyth to Rolfe Street station in Smethwick by this method, and were even told by a guard that we had to change trains in Shrewsbury. To get off the station we just told the ticket collector that we had got on at West Brom, the charge, 7d each. In this instance, to get on the train in Aberystwyth we had sneaked through the freight yard gates. Due to the conductors there was no way we could get there for nothing if we had to go by bus.

Despite a dull school trip several years before, here Graham Twist and Alec Moss are back in Aberystwyth in 1958, the days of 'free' train journeys.

There was something wonderful about flying down country lanes as fast as you could on your racing bike. The freedom of the open road certainly applied as far as we were concerned. We would get to wherever the job was and then spend all day loading the roof with tiles. This meant carrying the tiles on your shoulder up a two-storey pole ladder and then up to the top of the roof. We always carried billycans in our knapsacks complete with tea and sugar and would simply nick a bottle of milk from any house doorstep on the way. To get hot water we would just chop up some of the roof laths or use the timber lying around to make a fire.

The tiles would come in all sizes, from the plain tile, a small one, to the pan tile, a really big one. Whatever they were it was our job to get them onto the roof. Most roof tilers back then would carry the tiles on their heads, but we would carry ours on our shoulders. I must admit I always had a sneaking regard for the head-carrying tilers. It was a hard day's graft followed by the ride home, and all for the magnificent sum of five bob a day. We carried our tools and sandwiches in our knapsacks, the tools consisting of a razor-sharp hatchet for chopping the laths, a couple of trowels, a knife, string line, nail bag and measuring tape. We once tiled a complete row of houses on the Queslett Road, on the left as you go towards the Aldridge Road. The cost of these houses was on a large billboard, the astronomical asking price? £1,250.

It was about this time, in early 1956, that we began to think of what we wanted to do when we left school – and because of my interest in the countryside I decided I wanted to work on a farm. Came the day we had to meet the bloke who was going to help us get the jobs we wanted and, as such, decide our futures.

'Name?'

I told him and he sorted out what was obviously a report of my now rapidly vanishing school life.

'What do you want to do lad?' (this said by the bloke with his head buried in a large notebook.)

'I want to work on a farm,' I said. At this he looked up.

'You want to work on a farm?'

'Yes.'

'You don't want to work on a farm, outside in all sorts of weather, clearing up pig, horse and cow shit. Working from dawn till dusk and sometimes later. No my boy what you need is a job close to home, where you will only have to work five-and-a-half days a week. Somewhere you can get to without catching the milk train.' He wrote something down in the notebook. 'When you leave I will get you an interview at a factory near where you live. A bit of advice, don't give the gaffer any lip and make sure your shoes are polished.' I looked down at my second-hand brown sandals with the middle strap missing and thought of the beltings I had had over the years for being a smart Alec, and all I could do was laugh and say 'yes sir.' My dreams of riding off, driving a huge herd of cattle into the sunset across a vast endless plain, ended in tatters. He got me an interview and consequently a job at the Norton Motorbike Company, and I hated every minute of it. But, as was so aptly said in *Gone with Wind*, 'tomorrow is another day.'

Acknowledgements

As with all works of this kind where the memory is put to the test, I, like everyone else, am to be found lacking in certain areas where memories and perceived memories merge. I wouldn't say I look back with rose-tinted glasses, but time certainly does colour and sometimes blur the past. Luckily for me, I am surrounded by people who also lived in my past – if not with me then certainly at the same time – you could say we lived different lives together.

Some of these people need a big thank you from me, for without them to remind me of things, to correct a memory or to add a fact or two, then this book about the backstreets of Aston would have been very hard to put together.

These people start with my wife, Sheila, whom I started to court in 1958 under the gas lamp at the bottom of her yard in Cowper Street. She has been a rock to me over all these years and has supported me and our family through all the good times but, more importantly, through the bad times too. She has taken pleasure in reminding me of her point of view of situations that developed our relationship, especially when it came to making me see the facts of things as they were and not as I wanted them to be. She is a true Brummie and from the best part of Birmingham – Aston.

Josie Moss (née Gillam) supplied photographs and memories of Alec, and reminded us both of things long forgotten: Josie and Alec were integral parts of our past and we spent many very happy times together.

My brother Terry's family, wife Alison and sons Gregory and Jason have supplied wonderful photos and precious memories of Terry. It is a tribute to Terry and Alison that both their sons have done well in their chosen careers

Graham Twist, Josie Gillam and Alec Moss outside the block of flats in Wyrley Birch, Erdington, in 1958. They moved us to this area when they started to pull Aston down.

– indeed Jason has been the World Champion pools player on two occasions – and I know my brother was immensely proud of them all.

Again my brother Harry and sister Valerie had an input into certain parts of this book, as did Harry's wife Lorraine and her mother Evelyn who is a marvel of memory about Aston and certainly the Newtown Row area and its many diverse shops and businesses. I hope the readers enjoy the 'monkey run' that Evelyn and her future husband, Harold, commonly known as 'Ted', trod all those years ago. I am sure there are things written here which readers will be able to contest as to which shop was where and what it was called, but as I said before, to write this book I have had to trawl my memory of sixty years ago, and if it makes you think and adjust the facts then obviously you are living the memory too, and can perhaps take pleasure as I do in recalling the past, warts and all.

Cousin June Christie and cousin Derek and his Phillips Street sweetheart Valerie also contributed, and for this I thank them. Brothers-in-law, Leo Bunting and John Gibbons and his wife Mary also need a mention for their support and recollections of the past. Tony Jordan and Joe Taft, both blasts from the past,

Terry with his landlady in Margate in 1960.

got in touch with me recently and provided both memories and photographs. Beryl Evans, ex-Summer Laner, has provided photographs, time and memories of both the school and the Aston area. I give her a real vote of thanks. Dr Carl Chinn has kindly once again allowed me to use some of his photographs of the Aston area from 'Birmingham Lives' (the Carl Chinn Archive), for which I am grateful. He has, as before, shown me support and encouragement in my writings and is always prompt in replying when I have asked him any questions. Michelle Tilling of The History Press deserves my thanks for being positive in all her dealings with me and for being understanding about my recent illness.

I must also thank the Queen Elizabeth Hospital in Edgbaston, for the real care and attention I have received from all the staff over the last two years. Without the life-saving surgery performed on me by Mr Tariq Ismail and his wonderful team, including all the departments that in my opinion performed above and beyond the call of duty, I would literally not be here today to tell this story. It is still an ongoing situation (ask the Chemo Team) but I rest easy at nights knowing I am under the wing of true, caring professionals.

To all the people above and to all my fellow Astonites and Brummies especially, I give my heartfelt thanks. Each in your own way has produced the nuts and bolts of this book – it only rested on me to put it together.